I0199003

THE BATTLE OF
PEA RIDGE

THE CIVIL WAR FIGHT FOR THE OZARKS

JAMES R. KNIGHT

SERIES EDITOR DOUGLAS BOSTICK

THE
History
PRESS

Published by The History Press
Charleston, SC 29403
www.historypress.net

Copyright © 2012 by James R. Knight
All rights reserved

Cover: *On the Battery*, Andy Thomas, artist, Carthage, Missouri,
www.andythomas.com.

First published 2012

ISBN 978-1-5402-0652-7

Library of Congress Cataloging-in-Publication Data

Knight, James R., 1945-
The Battle of Pea Ridge : the Civil War fight for the Ozarks / James R. Knight.
pages cm. -- (History Press Civil War sesquicentennial series)
Includes bibliographical references and index.
ISBN 978-1-5402-0652-7
1. Pea Ridge, Battle of, Ark., 1862. I. Title.
E473.17.K58 2012
973.7'31--dc23
2011051847

Notice: The information in this book is true and complete to the best of our knowledge. It is offered without guarantee on the part of the author or The History Press. The author and The History Press disclaim all liability in connection with the use of this book.

All rights reserved. No part of this book may be reproduced or transmitted in any form whatsoever without prior written permission from the publisher except in the case of brief quotations embodied in critical articles and reviews.

Dedicated to my great-grandfather, Third Sergeant James R. Knight, Company I, Fourth Arkansas Infantry (CSA), who marched into the Ozarks with Earl Van Dorn, walked back over the Boston Mountains to the Arkansas River Valley after the battle was lost and lived to tell the tale.

Contents

CONTENTS

Preface

This book, my third contribution to The History Press's Civil War Sesquicentennial Series, is the most personal. I grew up in northwest Arkansas about seventy-five miles from the Pea Ridge Battlefield. My paternal great-grandfather and namesake, to whom it is dedicated, was in the Fourth Arkansas Infantry (CSA), which fought in Morgan's Woods. When the Confederates retreated back to the camps along Frog Bayou, some of them occupied land farmed by my maternal great-great-grandfather—land on which my mother still lives. He later enlisted in the Confederate army and was with General John S. Marmaduke at Prairie Grove.

Although many sources were used, the foundation for this story is a benchmark work on the Pea Ridge Campaign, *Pea Ridge: Civil War Campaign in the West*, by William L. Shea and Earl J. Hess. Professor Shea was very kind in encouraging me to go forward with this work and in answering questions along the way. His and Mr. Hess's work is referenced in my notes many times, but it should be understood that, even if not specifically noted, their work continually informed my understanding of the events as nothing else could. Without their work, this book would never have happened.

The other critical source for this work was Hal Jespersen, who created a new series of maps for the book. In a campaign and battle as complex as Pea Ridge, good maps are essential for the reader to follow the action. Without Hal's agreement to work with me, I probably wouldn't have taken on the project. It's safe to say that he exceeded all of my expectations. Thanks, Hal, for your skill and patience.

Finally, every military historian knows that nothing can take the place of walking the ground. My thanks to the staff at Pea Ridge National Military Park and Chief Interpreter Troy Banzhaf, who took several hours to show me the battlefield that, in many ways, is little changed from that time 150 years ago.

As always, thanks to Doug Bostick and the folks at The History Press for giving an old history geek one more chance.

Prologue

"To make a reputation and serve my country conspicuously…or fail."[1]
—*Earl Van Dorn*

Pocahontas, Arkansas
February 22, 1862
Headquarters, Trans-Mississippi District No. 2
Major General Earl Van Dorn (CSA) commanding

On this morning, the commander of all Confederate forces in Louisiana north of the Red River, as well as Arkansas, Indian Territory and most of Missouri, sat in his headquarters in this little northeast Arkansas town planning his grand offensive to march north the following month and capture St. Louis. To most observers, Earl Van Dorn would have seemed the very picture of mid-nineteenth-century southern manhood—the cultured gentleman, the dashing cavalier and the natural-born warrior all rolled into one. At five-foot-eight, with sandy hair and piercing blue eyes, he made a strong impression on the men he commanded, as well as on the many beautiful women who crossed his path—a fact that was not at all lost on him. Consequently, he had a well-earned reputation as an aggressive—some would say rash—commander, as well as something of a ladies' man.

Earl Van Dorn was born in Port Gibson, Mississippi, on September 17, 1820, the fourth of nine children of Peter and Sophia Van Dorn. Growing up as a son of the plantation aristocracy, he was superbly connected both socially and politically to the antebellum southern power structure. Jefferson Davis, the future Confederate president, was a neighbor and family friend, and when eighteen-year-old Earl decided that he wanted to be a soldier, he received an "at large" appointment to West Point for the class beginning in the summer of 1838, arranged by his great-uncle, former president Andrew Jackson.

Although he graduated from West Point in the summer of 1842, "Buck" Van Dorn, as he was known to his classmates, had not been a model cadet, placing fourth from the bottom of his class of fifty-six but still two places ahead of another cadet bound for great things: James Longstreet of Georgia. All told, Van Dorn's class would eventually produce seventeen general officers for one side or the other in the coming Civil War. Van Dorn had served with some distinction as a junior officer in the Mexican-America War, but unlike many of his fellow West Pointers who had resigned for more lucrative jobs in the civilian world after the war, Van Dorn stayed on. Now, as the new Confederate departmental commander, he could look back on almost twenty years of military service.

For the last few years before the Civil War, Van Dorn had served mainly in Texas with the famous Second Cavalry, commanded by Albert S. Johnston and then Robert E. Lee. Combat on the frontier in the years leading up to the war usually meant protecting settlers, staging small unit raids on villages and chasing roaming bands of Indians whose first instinct was to scatter and run. Van Dorn had several encounters with Comanches and was once seriously wounded by arrows, so his personal courage was never in doubt. The problem with bringing that kind of combat experience to the current conflict, however, was that the forces opposing him in the Civil War seldom fought like Indians, and his own army of foot soldiers, artillery and supply wagons could seldom live off the land or be maneuvered like a troop of frontier cavalry.

When the state of Mississippi seceded in January 1861, there was no doubt where Earl Van Dorn's allegiances lay. He resigned from the U.S. Army, went back home and was immediately commissioned one of four brigadier generals of the Mississippi Militia, but he didn't intend to stay there. By March, he had traded his militia rank for a colonel's commission in the regular Confederate army, and because of his prior service there, he was sent back to Texas to try and recruit men from the Federal forces still in the state. By September, Van Dorn was back in Richmond, where his old friend, Jefferson Davis, commissioned him a major general and sent him to command a division in Joseph E. Johnston's Army of the Potomac. Even though he was now a major general, being in an army with two full generals—P.G.T. Beauregard and Johnston—meant that Van Dorn was still a second-tier player, but that changed when he was ordered back to Richmond in early January 1862 and given command of the Trans-Mississippi Department.

Ever since the war started, the Confederacy had been struggling to organize and equip its army. With the enemy's capital and main army barely one hundred miles from Richmond in Washington, D.C., the Confederate forces in Virginia had first priority. Farther west, they had to rely more on state militia and arsenals for men and arms. This caused a fair amount of friction between the government in Richmond, which wished to muster many of these state troops and their arms into the Confederate army, and the state governors, who wanted to continue controlling their own militia. In the Confederate states west of the Mississippi River, the problem was complicated by the distance and the difficulty of timely communications.

In the summer of 1861, the main Confederate army in the Arkansas/ Missouri/Indian Territory area was located in northwest Arkansas and was commanded by Brigadier General Benjamin McCulloch, a former Texas Ranger and practically a legend in his adopted state. Across the line in Missouri, the pro-Southern forces called themselves the Missouri State Guard and were commanded by Sterling Price, a major general in the state militia. These two forces had managed to come together temporarily—and contentiously—long enough to beat Union general Nathaniel Lyon at Wilson's Creek in August, but just as quickly, McCulloch and the Confederates then marched back to Arkansas, and there matters stood in the Ozarks until Earl Van Dorn entered the picture a few weeks before the start of our story.

In spite of being seven hundred miles away from Richmond on the far side of the Mississippi, the state of Missouri was vitally important to the Confederacy—gaining control of its resources and manpower would be a huge advantage. Both Missouri and Arkansas were originally part of General Albert Sidney Johnston's department, but by early 1862, President Davis had decided to make a change. In spite of their victory at Wilson's Creek, McCulloch and Price had continued to squabble over each other's authority. McCulloch believed that his brigadier's commission in the regular Confederate army should outrank Price's major general rank in the Missouri State Guard. Not surprisingly, Price disagreed. Davis's solution to the impasse was to create a new Trans-Mississippi Department and place over them both a Confederate major general—a West Pointer who would add the professional military background that both McCulloch and Price lacked.

Earl Van Dorn was not Davis's first choice. It was only after Henry Heth and Braxton Bragg turned down the appointment that Van Dorn got the call, but an independent departmental command was what he had been anticipating. Van Dorn arrived in Little Rock and took command on January 29; he spent the next three weeks planning his spring offensive. He had written to Price in Springfield that he would be reinforced and that the offensive would begin on March 20 with at least fifteen thousand men. The message Van Dorn received on February 22, however, changed everything. The note reported that a Union army had pushed Price out of Springfield ten days earlier and that he had been falling back ever since. Price's Missouri State Guard was now settling into a winter camp south of Fayetteville, Arkansas, across a ridgeline from Benjamin McCulloch's Confederate army.

After the initial shock of the message, Van Dorn began to see this development as an opportunity in disguise. The main Federal army in southwest Missouri had unintentionally concentrated Van Dorn's forces for him by driving Price and the Missouri State Guard into Arkansas and into the arms of McCulloch's Confederate army. That Federal army now sat in camp about fifteen miles north of Fayetteville, with only one road connecting it to its support back in Missouri. With the combined forces of Price and McCulloch, Van Dorn now had a chance to destroy this Federal army. That would make him the master of northwest Arkansas and southwest Missouri and put him well on his way to his dream of capturing St. Louis—just from a slightly different direction. He made plans to leave immediately for the Confederate camps, more than two hundred miles away, to lead his new army in person. Finally, here was the chance to make the reputation for which had always dreamed.[2]

—m—

Cross Hollow, Arkansas (fifteen miles north of Fayetteville)
February 22, 1862
Headquarters, Federal Army of the Southwest
Brigadier General Samuel R. Curtis (USA) commanding

As Earl Van Dorn read his messages this morning at his headquarters in eastern Arkansas, two hundred miles to the west, the commander of the Federal Army of the Southwest sat in his tent in this former Confederate camp, trying to enjoy the warmer weather and pondering his situation. Brigadier General Samuel Curtis and his army of just over ten thousand men sat about seventeen miles south of the Missouri border in northwest Arkansas. About thirty miles in his front sat a Confederate army that now numbered almost seventeen thousand men. His single supply line stretched back to the railhead at Rolla, Missouri, so every pound of food and every round of ammunition had to be hauled in wagons over almost two hundred miles of primitive road, and his odds for any significant reinforcement were nil. All in all, his was a precarious position. The Federal commander of the Army of the Southwest was in danger of becoming a victim of his own success.

Born in New York State, Samuel Ryan Curtis was an 1831 graduate of West Point, but like many other academy graduates in the early nineteenth century, he did not make the military a career. He spent a year at a primitive post in Indian Territory and then resigned to become a civil engineer and attorney. Curtis was living in Ohio when the Mexican-American War broke out and commanded the Second Regiment of the state's volunteers in Zachary Taylor's army but saw no combat. Instead, he was assigned to administer several captured cities. After returning from Mexico, he settled in Iowa and moved into politics in the mid-1850s, becoming the mayor of Keokuk and then one of the first members of the new Republican Party to be elected to Congress in 1856.

With the beginning of the Civil War, Curtis came home from Washington, raised the Second Iowa Regiment and was elected its colonel. Soon after, however, he was promoted to brigadier general and moved to District Headquarters in St. Louis.

Curtis, an honest man and an able administrator, was not impressed with the graft and inefficiency that pervaded the department being run by his commander, Major General John C. Fremont. Eventually, the defeat of Brigadier General Nathaniel Lyon at Wilson's Creek in August and clashes with President Lincoln's policies led to General Fremont's removal in November, and it was Fremont's replacement, Major General Henry W. Halleck, who finally gave Samuel Curtis his first combat command—thirty years after West Point.

When Halleck took over in St. Louis, he immediately began to clean up the administrative mess that Fremont had left and plan a spring offensive against the Confederates in Kentucky and Tennessee using the Ohio, Cumberland, Tennessee and Mississippi Rivers. Before he could start in on the Confederates across the Mississippi, however, there was a problem there in Missouri that Halleck had to settle.

Back in July, pro-Union forces had held a convention and ousted the elected governor, Claiborne F. Jackson, who was deemed too pro-secession, and the army then drove Jackson and the other pro-Confederate elected legislators out of the capital and into the southwestern part of the state. Jackson and the other pro-Confederate politicians were, however, supported by the Missouri State Guard, commanded by Major General Sterling Price, a Mexican-American War veteran and former governor. Price and his men were barely trained and poorly supplied, but with the help of Confederate forces from Arkansas, they had defeated the Union forces at Wilson's Creek in August and had been raiding in the central part of the state, all the way to the Missouri River, ever since.

Ragtag though they were, the members of the Missouri State Guard were getting better organized and better armed with every capture of enemy stores and every confrontation with the Federal troops—with more Confederate sympathizers were joining them every day. Henry Halleck was, above all, a careful man, and he did not intend to launch his spring offensive with such an enemy force within the state that would tie up troops and resources better used in Tennessee, so Price and his men had to be either destroyed or driven out of the state. That was the job he gave to Samuel Curtis.

Curtis arrived at Rolla, Missouri, the day after Christmas with orders to assume command of all the troops assembling there, and he immediately ran into problems. The officer then in command was Brigadier General Franz Sigel, who protested the order and resigned rather than be demoted to division commander. Since many of the men in Sigel's command were German immigrants, as was Sigel himself, this was no small matter. There was a public outcry and some anxious moments within the large German immigrant community in St. Louis, but in the end Sigel was persuaded to withdraw his resignation and serve as Curtis's second in command.

Due to unforeseen circumstances, General Halleck was forced to begin his Tennessee offensive sooner than he had planned, with Brigadier General Ulysses S. Grant and his troops leaving Cairo, Illinois, on February 2. Eight days later, Curtis began to move from Lebanon, Missouri, toward Price's winter quarters in Springfield, forty-five miles away. On February 12, with Curtis only a few miles away, Price decided to withdraw rather than try to hold Springfield with his outnumbered and ill-equipped forces.

For the last ten days, Price and Curtis had been involved in a running fight as Price and his men marched south into Arkansas, with Curtis and the Federal army nipping at their heels all the way. Now the two armies had settled in, with Price camped with McCulloch's men in the relative safety of the Boston Mountains south of Fayetteville and Curtis occupying the old Confederate camp at Cross Hollow. Curtis had a decision to make: should he stay in northwest Arkansas at the end of his tenuous, two-hundred-mile-long supply line and risk being cut off by a superior Confederate force, or should he fall back into the relative safety of Missouri and declare his mission accomplished?[3]

Over the next two weeks, Samuel Curtis and Earl Van Dorn would determine who would control northwest Arkansas and southwest Missouri for the rest of the war. It would be two and a half years before Sterling Price again led Confederate troops on Missouri soil, and when he did, he would once again face Samuel Curtis—with the same result.

Chapter 1

Arkansas in 1861

Most of the men in the Federal army who marched into northwest Arkansas in February 1862 were midwesterners—men at home on the prairies of Illinois and Iowa. To these boys, many away from home for the first time, the sparsely settled Ozark Mountains, with its stony hills and steep valleys crossed by uncounted small streams, were unlike any place they had ever seen, and at first, this new country seemed exotic and beautiful. To one officer, Arkansas was "a wonderful change of scenery to the boys from the Illinois prairies," and to another soldier, it was "the most beautiful scenery I ever beheld in my life."[4] After living, marching and fighting there for a few weeks, however, their opinions began to change.

One thing that impressed all the flatland farm boys in Samuel Curtis's army about north Arkansas was the universal presence and unending supply of rocks. One soldier wrote home that "the ground is covered with stones from the size of a pea up to cliffs of two hundred feet in height of solid rock," while another described the Ozark Plateau as "composed of millions of little rocks thrown together in one huge pile." After spending several months in north Arkansas and southern Missouri, one soldier from Illinois gave his impression by writing, "Of all the country that I have ever seen, for sterility and rockiness, this takes the rag off the bush." Almost at a loss for words, an Indiana soldier summed it up by saying that he and the Federal army were lost in "one of the most rantankerous [sic], half manufactured sections of the country you ever saw."[5]

Neither were the midwesterners much impressed with the local inhabitants. One Federal staff officer wrote home that northern Arkansas was "very thinly settled by a wild semi-civilized race of backwoodsmen." Another concluded that Arkansas was "decidedly a land of corn dodgers and poor fiddlers." An Indiana cavalryman wrote home, trying to describe the people he was seeing on his way through Arkansas to his fiancée. If his grammar left a little to be desired, his feelings were clear enough. "You have often read and heard tell of the curious ways that the people have in this state, but the stories was never bad enough to be true."[6]

Arkansas certainly was, in many ways, the backwater of the Confederacy. Except for tiny Florida, it was the least populated Confederate state and was basically tied with Tennessee for having the lowest percentage of its population as slaves. If the soldiers' impressions of mountainous northern Arkansas were generally true, the eastern part of the state had more in common with its neighbors to the east and south—Mississippi and Louisiana. There were large plantations along the Mississippi River and large cotton fields worked by slaves.

After the formation of the Confederate government in February, Arkansas, like several other Southern states, called a convention to decide whether to join. The newly elected governor, Henry M. Rector, supported the Confederate cause, but even with his influence, the Unionists were too strong and the convention failed to recommend secession but did agree to put the question to the people during a general election in August. All of that changed with the firing on Fort Sumter and Lincoln's call for troops from the state to put down the rebellion.

Even for many of the Union men, sending Arkansas troops to fight other Southerners in South Carolina was just too much. The Secession Convention was recalled and voted again. This time, there was only one delegate who refused to make the vote unanimous. Arkansas seceded on May 6, 1861, and was accepted into the Confederacy two weeks later.[7] Many who voted for secession took no joy in it, however. Jesse Turner, a Union delegate and opponent of slavery, nonetheless voted for secession, telling a friend that it was a "sad and deplorable necessity, but unavoidable under the circumstances." To his wife, he confided: "Would to God that it could have been otherwise…The people of the state demanded it…God knows what is to become of our unhappy country. All is darkness and gloom ahead."[8]

Whatever the feelings of the individuals involved, it was done, and Arkansas began to prepare for war. The Federal arsenal in Little Rock had passed into state hands peaceably in February, and the arsenal at Fort Smith followed in April, but the stores they contained would become a point of contention between governor Rector and the Confederate government.

Rector used many of the weapons from the arsenals to arm state militia units that came under his control, leaving few for the Confederate troops to be raised in the state. For the rest of this first year of the war, the tension between state authority and Confederate authority would surface many times. To command the Confederate forces in northwest Arkansas and Indian Territory, President Jefferson Davis turned to a Tennessean who, ironically enough, had spent the last twenty years fighting Indians in Texas.

Benjamin McCulloch was born in Rutherford County, Tennessee, in 1811 and went to Texas in early 1836, following his friend and neighbor David Crockett. Only a case of measles saved McCulloch from joining Crockett and the others at the Alamo. For the next twenty-five years, McCulloch fought with Sam Houston at San Jacinto, was a frontier surveyor and Indian fighter and Texas Ranger, was a member of the Texas legislature, was Zachary Taylor's chief of scouts in the Mexican-American War, was a gold prospector and sheriff in California and was the United States marshal for the Eastern District of Texas. By the time the Civil War came to Texas, Ben McCulloch was already a legend in the state.

Soon after Texas seceded, McCulloch was commissioned a colonel in the Confederate army and led the troops who captured General David E. Twiggs and the Union forces at San Antonio. On May 11, McCulloch became the first civilian to be commissioned a general officer in the Confederate army, with the assignment of securing northwest Arkansas and the Indian Territory. Arriving in Little Rock, he found that most of the arms taken with the Federal arsenal had already been passed out by state officials and were "scattered over the state in every direction."[9]

McCulloch moved on up the Arkansas River to Fort Smith, where he set up a camp of instruction that he named Camp Walker. According to an observer, McCulloch and his small staff arrived at Fort Smith "without a dollar, a man, or a gun," According to another, "[H]e came unannounced, without bluster, fuss or feathers, in the garb of an earnest citizen who meant business." There, in May 1861, on the border with Indian Territory, he began to build an army.[10]

Starting almost from scratch, McCulloch had the beginnings of a credible force in northwest Arkansas by the end of June. The nucleus of his army was the Third Louisiana infantry regiment, commanded by Colonel Louis Hebert and sent from New Orleans to help guard the state from attack from north of the Red River. Arriving at Fort Smith on June 7, the Third Louisiana numbered 1,085 officers and men. In the coming months, they would march and fight over terrain like nothing they had ever seen near New Orleans or Baton Rouge, but through it all, they would be McCulloch's best.[11] Also in June, two mounted units were formed—the First and Second Arkansas Mounted Rifles—giving McCulloch the beginnings of a cavalry force. The First was commanded by Colonel Thomas J. Churchill and the Second by Colonel James M. McIntosh (West Point class of 1849). Eventually, several Texas cavalry units would also join them.

At the end of May, McCulloch and Albert Pike began a recruiting trip through the Indian nations. They received a favorable reception from the Choctaws, the Chickasaws and the Creeks, but the Cherokees were more difficult. By the end of July, however, Stands Watie had recruited a unit of Cherokees, and a second one would be raised in the coming months.

Brigadier General Albert Pike, commander of the Cherokee, Creek, Choctaw and Chickasaw Indian troops at Leetown. *Courtesy of the Library of Congress.*

In early July, McCulloch began moving his forces north from Fort Smith in response to a call for help from Missouri. Governor Jackson and all of the pro-Confederate state representatives had been ousted from the state capitol by Union forces and were falling back toward Neosho, along with part of the Missouri State Guard, and were being pursued by several thousand Federal troops. To McCulloch, the situation was serious, but Missouri was out of his jurisdiction. In late June, however, he was given permission to cross over into the state and help. In response to the emergency, about one thousand men of the Arkansas State Militia went with McCulloch as well.[12]

For the next month, McCulloch and his men, along with the poorly organized and poorly armed Missouri State Guard under Sterling Price, held off the Federal troops, allowing Governor Jackson to set up a sort of government in exile in Neosho, and finally defeated the Federal forces at Wilson's Creek on August 10, killing General Nathaniel Lyon. After Wilson's Creek, however, McCulloch soon took his men back to Arkansas, where he began to reorganize and train them.

Area of operations—southwest Missouri and northwest Arkansas 1861–62. *Courtesy of Hal Jespersen.*

By mid-September, McCulloch was off to the north again, this time heading for Kansas, but his army was stopped by an epidemic of measles and then sidetracked by the advance of another Federal army in southwest Missouri. Finally, in late November, McCulloch brought his army back to Arkansas and into camp at Cross Hollow, astride Telegraph Road about seventeen miles south of the Missouri border and fifteen miles north of Fayetteville. By the end of November, the army was settling into winter quarters. Hebert's Third Louisiana infantry stayed near Cross Hollow, while the mounted units under James McIntosh came down out of the Boston Mountains and wintered along Frog Bayou near the Arkansas River, just northeast of Van Buren.

Having made arrangements for his men, McCulloch passed command to James McIntosh and departed for Richmond. During the past seven months, McCulloch had been forced to operate almost on his own because of the difficulty in communicating with his superiors almost one thousand miles away. Because of his relative isolation, McCulloch felt that many false impressions had developed about him due to the biased reports of others. Most of these were born out of his difficulties in operating with Sterling Price and his Missouri State Guard, which McCulloch considered little better than a poorly armed rabble. Now that winter had come, it was time to consult the leaders in Richmond face to face and clear up some things if the coming year was to be better than the current one.

Chapter 2

Missouri in 1861

U nlike its smaller and, in many ways, more primitive neighbor to the south, Missouri was not a backwater state in any sense of the word. St. Louis in the east was the commercial center of the Upper Mississippi Valley and home to a large immigrant community—mostly German and Irish. In the west, Independence and St. Joseph were the gateways to the westward expansion. In industry, resources and transportation, Missouri in 1861 equaled all the other Confederate states in Trans-Mississippi combined. In addition to its strategic and economical importance to both North and South, Missouri had been at the center of the debate on slavery since its admission as a state forty years earlier.

Missouri was initially settled primarily by people from slaveholding states like Tennessee, Kentucky and Virginia, so the institution had been a part of the territory from the beginning. In 1819, when a bill was introduced in Congress to allow Missouri to draft a constitution and apply to be admitted as a state, the balance in Congress between slave states and free states was even at eleven each. To admit Missouri as a slave state would upset the balance. That was solved by admitting Maine as a free state, keeping the balance, but the larger question concerning Missouri's admission as a slave state had to do with the future of slavery in the new territories.

Missouri was the first state to be carved entirely out of the Louisiana Purchase, and the guidelines agreed on by Congress were collectively called the Missouri Compromise.[13] It was decided that Missouri would be admitted as a slave state and Maine as a free state but that, in the future, the line of 36′ 30″ north latitude—the southern boundary of Missouri—would be the boundary between slave and free states created from the new territory. By 1861, however, the Missouri Compromise had broken down, and it started on Missouri's western border.

In 1854, the Kansas-Nebraska Act became law. It organized the two territories and put them on the path to statehood, but more importantly, it contained a provision that allowed each territory to decide for itself whether to come into the Union as a free state or slave state. Since both of these potential new states were above the 36′ 30″ north latitude line, they should have been required to be free states. Allowing the states to choose their status as slave or free essentially nullified the Missouri Compromise. Not surprisingly, most southerners in Congress supported the measure, since it gave them at least the possibility of expanding slavery in all of the new territories. Most northerners, of course, opposed it for allowing just that possibility.

The Kansas-Nebraska Act fractured the Democratic Party into northern and southern factions and was directly responsible for the rise of the new Republican Party that fielded its first presidential and Congressional candidates two years later. It also kicked off a conflict along the Kansas/Missouri border that would continue until it was swallowed up by the Civil War. Proslavery forces in western Missouri began to push into Kansas, hoping to tip the balance of any election toward slavery. Abolitionist groups in the east began recruiting settlers to move to Kansas to counteract the proslavery element and tip any election in *their* favor, and very soon, violence broke out, with both sides blaming the other. Cross-border raids became common, and before long, the new territory became known as "Bleeding Kansas," for good reason. When the Civil War came to Missouri in 1861, many folks in the western part of the state had already been fighting it for several years.

The election of 1860 brought the new Republican Party to power with Abraham Lincoln of Illinois, but in Missouri, Claiborne F. Jackson, a Douglas Democrat, won the governor's race easily. With family in both Kentucky and Virginia, Jackson sympathized with the South, as did many of the state legislators, but he did not openly advocate secession like the governors of several other uncommitted southern states. Even so, in his inaugural address, he called for a convention to decide how the state would address the reality of the new Confederate states, just as the other uncommitted southern states had done.

Missouri's convention met on February 28 and elected Sterling Price its president. On March 9, it resolved that there was not adequate cause to withdraw from the Union. It also rejected an amendment that would have bound the state to secede if the other uncommitted border states did. For the time being, Missouri would bide its time and hope for a peaceful resolution between North and South, but like in the other uncommitted southern states, the attack on Fort Sumter and Lincoln's call for troops changed everything.

Lincoln's April 15 call for seventy-five thousand men to put down the rebellion forced the remaining southern and border states to finally choose sides. The governors of Arkansas, Missouri, Kentucky, Tennessee, Virginia and North Carolina all refused to furnish troops, with Governor Jackson saying that Missouri would not furnish one man "to carry on such an unholy crusade."[14] Within two months, Arkansas, Tennessee, Virginia and North Carolina had passed ordinances of secession, but Kentucky and Missouri had decided to adopt a position of "armed neutrality." Kentucky would be able to maintain this rather self-contradictory position for about four months, but Missouri's position would deteriorate much sooner.

If Governor Jackson and Sterling Price were the leaders of the pro-Southern faction, the most powerful man in the pro-Union camp was a man named Francis P. Blair Jr. A Princeton-educated lawyer from Kentucky, Blair advocated emancipating Missouri's slaves and converting it to a free state. He was a founder of the new Republican Party and was the chairman of the House Military Affairs committee in Lincoln's first Congress. Blair was committed to seeing Missouri stay in the Union—by force, if necessary.

During the 1860 election, Blair had organized Republican support in St. Louis' large German community by forming clubs called the "Wide Awakes," and now, in early 1861, these clubs began to secretly drill as a "Home Guard." On the pro-Southern side, groups were also forming quasi-military minuteman units, and both sides had the same objective in mind. In St. Louis sat the largest arsenal west of the Mississippi River, with enough small arms to outfit several divisions and enough gunpowder to blow up half the city. The pro-Southern men were making plans to capture the arsenal, and Blair and his men were determined to protect it for the Union.

The battle for the St. Louis arsenal was never an even contest. While the pro-Southern forces had to organize from scratch with enthusiastic but mostly untrained civilians, Blair, with his seat in Congress and the ear of President Lincoln, could in addition to his Home Guard call on regular army troops to protect what was, after all, Federal property. To this end, Blair used his influence to get the army to transfer a company of regulars from Fort

Riley, Kansas, to St. Louis in February 1861. Its captain turned out to be the man who, probably more than any other, would push Missouri into the war.

Nathaniel Lyon was just what Frank Blair was looking for. Born in Connecticut and a descendant of Puritans, Lyon graduated from West Point in 1841. Lyon was a twenty-year veteran and a staunch Unionist and abolitionist who had just spent the last few years seeing "Bleeding Kansas" up close. Lyon had no intention of compromising, personally or professionally, with Southern sympathizers, whom he considered no better than traitors.

Soon after Governor Jackson's reply to Lincoln, he called the Missouri legislature into special session to enact measures to raise and equip a militia for the defense of the state. In line with his true sympathies, he also secretly sent a letter to President Davis asking the Confederacy to supply some cannons to help in capturing the St. Louis arsenal. It seems clear that, even at this time, Jackson considered secession inevitable. Five days later, a group of Southern sympathizers seized the small Federal arsenal at Liberty, in western Missouri. Militarily, its four obsolete brass cannons and small number of old flintlocks were insignificant, but it served to raise the temperature and strengthen Blair and Lyon and the the Unionists' call for more help from Washington.

One of the biggest obstacles to Blair and Lyon's plans was Lyon's own commander, Major General William S. Harney, who was too conservative and conciliatory, in their opinion. Two days after Lincoln's call for troops, Blair returned from Washington with authorization to arm five thousand "loyal citizens"—Blair's Home Guard—from stores at the arsenal. Since this completely bypassed Harney, he protested the order and was called to Washington for consultations. This left Lyon in temporary charge, which suited him and Blair perfectly. Soon after Harney's departure, Lyon received authorization from Washington to increase the enlistments up to ten thousand.

In the middle of Blair and Lyon's efforts on the Union side, Governor Jackson ordered a "training camp" set up outside St. Louis for the state militia, likely with hopes of capturing the arsenal. On May 8, four artillery pieces, provided by the Confederate government at Governor Jackson's request, were smuggled ashore, but it was too late. Lyon had armed about nine thousand men and then sent the rest of the arms across the river to Alton, Illinois. On May 10, Lyon surrounded the camp and took the state militiamen, commanded by General Daniel M. Frost, prisoner. As Lyon marched the militiamen through the streets of St. Louis, violence broke out as the crowds began to throw rocks and bricks. Inevitably, someone fired on the soldiers, and the troops replied. When it was finally over, almost one hundred people had been injured and twenty-eight had been killed. Present in the crowd were three men destined to become famous Civil War generals: Ulysses S. Grant, William T. Sherman and Sterling Price.

The incident at Camp Jackson, as the militia camp was called, touched off a flurry of activity. The legislature, meeting at Jefferson City, immediately passed bills dissolving the state militia and establishing a new organization called the Missouri State Guard. Sterling Price was named to head it and began organizing immediately. In the middle of all of this, General Harney returned from Washington. On May 21, Harney and Price met and concluded an agreement meant to defuse the situation, with Missouri maintaining its "armed neutrality." It's doubtful that either side really believed that the agreement was viable, but it gave Jackson, Price and the pro-Confederates three more weeks to prepare.

By the end of May, Blair had managed to get Harney relieved and Lyon appointed in his place, and on June 11, another meeting was held. Price and Governor Jackson met Nathaniel Lyon (now a brigadier general) and Frank Blair in St. Louis. After about four hours, Lyon simply announced that, since Missouri's elected leaders did not intend to cooperate fully with the Federal government in Washington, as the other "loyal" states were doing, it meant war. Lyon walked out of the meeting, and Jackson and Price caught the first train back to Jefferson City, cutting telegraph wires and burning bridges as they went. Jackson called for fifty thousand volunteers to join the State Guard and repel the "invasion," while Lyon telegraphed Washington asking for more troops to put down the "rebellion."

With the resources of the Federal government behind him, Lyon had the upper hand—at least at first. Four days after the St. Louis meeting, Lyon landed about two thousand men at Jefferson City to find Governor Jackson, the State Guard and most of the legislature gone. Over the next month, Lyon's troops and State Guard units would fight a series of skirmishes as the pro-Confederate group fell back into southwest Missouri. Finally, on July 5, the State Guard met a Federal force under Franz Sigel just north of Carthage and sent it back toward Springfield. The next day, the State Guard troops were joined by General Price and Confederate troops from Arkansas under General McCulloch.

While all of the marching and fighting had been going on, Unionists had reconvened the state convention. Since almost all of the Southern sympathizers were on their way into virtual exile, they had no trouble declaring the office of governor vacant. They then disbanded the legislature and set themselves up as the government of the state. The convention, dominated by Unionists, would rule the state under virtual marshal law for the next three years.

For the next three weeks, the State Guard settled in southwest of Neosho, McCulloch's Confederates moved back into Arkansas near Bentonville and General Lyon and the Federals went into camp at Springfield. By the end of the month, however, the Southern forces would be on the move again. After being on the run from the Federals for several weeks, Sterling Price and his Missouri State Guard were anxious for a chance to strike back.[15]

Chapter 3

"Seeing the Elephant"

Wilson's Creek

Camp on Sugar Creek, near Bentonville, Arkansas
July 18, 1861
Headquarters, McCulloch's Brigade

B rigadier General Ben McCulloch sat at his camp on the banks of this pretty little creek just a few miles south of the Missouri state line, planning his next move and writing a report to his superiors in Richmond. He and his men had come down here after a small skirmish near Neosho, which ended the Federal pursuit and left Governor Jackson and the pro-Southern legislature safe for the moment. Sterling Price and the State Guard were now camped at Cowskin Prairie, about thirty miles to the west, and General Nicholas B. Pearce, with about 2,500 Arkansas militiamen, was about twenty-five miles away at Maysville, on the border with Indian Territory. The Federals under Nathaniel Lyon had concentrated at Springfield and were fortifying the town.

McCulloch's first inclination was to go after the Federals at Springfield, but there was one major factor holding him back. In explaining his delay, his report notes, in part:

> *I am anxious to march against them* [Union troops under Lyon],
> *and if all of the available force now near me could be depended upon I*
> *think we could with success, or at least cut them off entirely from their*
> *supplies and re-enforcements; but upon consulting with General Price,*

in command of the Missouri forces, I find that his force of 8,000 or 9,000 men is badly organized, badly armed, and now almost entirely out of ammunition. This force was made by the concentration of different commands under their own generals. The consequence is that there is no concert of action among them, and will not be until a competent military man is put in command of the entire force. Under these circumstances I do not think that there is any disposition on the part of the Missourians to advance until they are better prepared.[16]

McCulloch was not impressed with what he saw of the Missouri State Guard or of its combat readiness at this point. He was wrong, however, about its leader's "disposition to advance," ready or not. Within a week, an agreement had been reached to unite all three forces at Cassville, Missouri, and then move the resulting army toward Springfield to confront the Federals there. At least in the case of the State Guard, there was really no other choice. After a couple of weeks at Cowskin Prairie, the men had just about exhausted the food and forage in the surrounding countryside and were soon going to have to move somewhere else or disband altogether. Moving toward the enemy was everybody's preference. Twelve days later, McCulloch sent another report to Richmond:

Headquarters McCulloch's Brigade,
Camp near Cassville, Mo., July 30, 1861.
Honorable L.P. Walker, Secretary of War, Richmond, Va.:

Sir: I have the honor to report that I am now at this place with my command on my way to Springfield. Since my communication of the 18th I have been busily engaged in preparing my force for a forward march, and have also been urging on the commanders of the different forces near me to be ready to co-operate with me.

By furnishing the Missouri force with all the ammunition I could spare, and also what could be spared from General Pearce's command, I have given them sufficient to warrant them in again taking the field. General Price, with his force of between 9,000 and 10,000 men, is encamped around Cassville. His effective force will hardly reach 7,000, and they are nearly all armed with shot-guns and common rifles. General Pearce, of Arkansas, is within 10 miles of Cassville with his command of 2,500 men. His infantry is well armed. My brigade is also near me amounting to about 3,200 nearly all well armed. I shall move towards

Springfield as rapidly as possible with the entire force, and hope soon to put the Missourians again in possession of it.[17]

Upon arriving at Cassville, Ben McCulloch found that things were already off to a bad start. Part of his agreement with General Price under which he began this march was that all the unarmed men and camp followers from the State Guard be left behind. At Cassville, however, he found them still following the Missouri troops. In spite of repeated promises from Price, the mob of "hangers on" was never left behind; as McCulloch had feared, the mob not only consumed already scarce rations but also became a real impediment when the shooting started. Price's inability or unwillingness to deal with this problem, plus the very poor performance of the State Guard's mounted troops under General Rains in the coming advance, did nothing to improve McCulloch's opinion of his Missouri allies.

On August 2, at a place called Dug Springs, Rains's cavalry ran into a small advance guard from the Federal army. According to one source, his men were routed by one cannonball and came fleeing back through the main body of the army in panic. Their only casualty was said to be a man who died of heatstroke. According to an officer in the Third Louisiana, this sorry episode caused McCulloch to "exhaust his entire vocabulary of vituperation (no meager one)."[18]

Overshadowing all of McCulloch's other concerns, however, was the command situation. Soon after the junction of the three forces at Cassville, it was decided that McCulloch should exercise overall command of the army. Whether the command was offered to McCulloch by Price voluntarily—as McCulloch and General Pearce claim—or was reluctantly given to him by General Price only after some harsh words were exchanged (and after McCulloch threatened to refuse to advance any farther), depends on whose story you believe.[19] However it came about, as the Southern forces approached Springfield, command of the entire force passed to General McCulloch.

As the Federal and Southern forces began to skirmish south of Springfield, one thing they had in common was an overestimation of their opponent's strength. Southern estimates consistently put Lyon's forces in and around Springfield at 10,000 to 12,000 men, whereas Lyon's own report of his strength six days before the battle was 5,868, with a fair number of his men soon coming to the end of their enlistments. The Federals, in their turn, estimated the enemy strength after the battle at 20,000 to 23,000, while McCulloch gave his effective strength, eleven days before the battle, as 12,700.

After the brief encounter at Dug Springs, McCulloch followed the Federals as they fell back toward Springfield but failed to catch them. Late on August 7, the advanced guard of the Southern forces arrived at Wilson's Creek, and by the next morning, the rest had come up and gone into camp on both sides of the stream. For the next two days, the army rested as the quartermasters struggled to bring up supplies and rations to replace the green corn that the men had been eating since they left Cassville. Meanwhile, General Price fumed at McCulloch for the delay and threatened to take back his Missourians and attack Lyon on his own. Although forced to cooperate on several occasions, the relationship between Price and McCulloch was always strained.

Finally, on August 9, McCulloch ordered an advance to begin at 9:00 p.m. so as to arrive at Springfield, about ten miles away, by sunrise the next morning, but he later countermanded the order when a light rain began to fall and more threatened. Most of the men did not have proper cartridge boxes and carried the paper cartridges in their pockets or in cloth bags. Marching the men in the rain would have almost guaranteed wet powder, reducing much of the army to sticks and stones. For an army that barely had twenty-five rounds per man as it was, McCulloch decided it was too big a risk.

In Springfield, General Lyon had been doing some planning of his own. He was convinced that he must retreat or be eventually encircled by McCulloch's larger army, but he had decided that he should hit it as heavy a blow as possible to discourage its pursuit. Accordingly, he started his men out from Springfield on that same Friday evening toward the Southern camps along Wilson's Creek. He, with the main force of about four thousand men, marched directly there, while Colonel Franz Sigel with one thousand men circled to the east so as to come in from the south. Had McCulloch not canceled the night march of his own army because of the rain, he and Lyon's men may well have met in the darkness of the early morning.

As it was, Lyon achieved almost complete surprise, hitting the Southern camps from two directions shortly after sunrise. At first, there was considerable confusion on the left among the Missourians as the unarmed men and the camp followers fled in panic from Lyon's regulars. After the initial shock, however, Price began to rally his armed units, and the fight on the Southerners' left settled into a close-range brawl.

Sterling Price may have been arrogant and difficult in his dealings with McCulloch, as well as impractical in his schemes of conquest, but on the battlefield leading his Missourians, he was fearless. For all the doubts General

McCulloch and others had voiced about the organization and leadership of the Missouri State Guard, once the battle was joined, the men stood their ground and fought every bit as bravely as the regular Confederate or Federal troops, and Lyon's attack was soon ground to a halt.

On the Southerners' right and rear, the smaller Federal force under Colonel Franz Sigel also had initial success, but General McCulloch soon formed his Third Louisiana Regiment along with some Arkansas troops and routed Sigel and his men, capturing three Federal cannons. With the threat on the right eliminated, McCulloch then turned his men to come to the aid of the Missourians, who were bearing the brunt of Lyon's attack.

On the slopes of what both sides came to call "Bloody Hill," the two sides fought all morning in a vicious, close-quarters struggle that one soldier described as "a private's battle" that was "akin to murder." After the war, that Missouri soldier wrote:

> [S]ome of the best blood in the land was being spilled as if it were ditch water. Lyon fought like a demon. Price charged time and again up the slope, only to be repulsed by the Federals lying on the crest. The Federals even more often broke over the crest of the hill and flowed down like an inundation of fire, and were thrown back.[20]

As noontime approached, the weight of Southern numbers began to tell, and then Brigadier General Nathaniel Lyon was killed. Upon Lyon's death, the Federal command fell to Major Samuel D. Sturgis. Unable to hear anything about the fate of Sigel's command and with his own men faint from thirst and almost out of ammunition, Sturgis ordered a withdrawal back to Springfield. Exhausted and almost out of ammunition themselves, the Southerners did not follow.[21] The next day, four companies of Texas scouts, sent by McCulloch to reconnoiter toward Springfield, found that the town had been evacuated. They raised the Third Texas Cavalry battle flag over the courthouse and waited for the rest of the army to arrive. For the moment, the Southern forces controlled all of southwestern Missouri.

Chapter 4

A Hollow Victory

S oon after the victory at Wilson's Creek, the relationship between McCulloch and Sterling Price became even more strained. Price took back control of his Missouri troops and planned an advance north to the Missouri River, but McCulloch refused to go along. He told Price that he did not believe he could stay on the Missouri River for long, with the Federals controlling both the railroads and the river traffic. In any case, McCulloch's assignment from the Confederate government was to protect Indian Territory and northwest Arkansas, and he was going back. Two weeks after the battle, he summed up his situation and his opinion of the Missouri forces in the following message to Richmond:

> *CAMP NEAR SPRINGFIELD, MO., August 24, 1861.*
> *His Excellency JEFFERSON DAVIS:*
>
> *The Arkansas troops have all [left] the service. Now only 3,000 troops are here…I am in no condition to advance, or even to meet an enemy here, having little ammunition or supplies of any kind. In fact, with the means of transportation now at my disposal I find it impossible to keep my force supplied, and will, in consequence, shorten my line, by falling back to the Arkansas line, near the Indiana Territory, and there proceed to drill and organize a force to meet the enemy when they take the field again in this quarter.*

We have little to hope or expect from the people of this State. The force now in the field is undisciplined and led by men who are mere politicians; not a soldier among them to control and organize this mass of humanity. The Missouri forces are in no condition to meet an organized army, nor will they ever be whilst under the present leaders. I dare not join them in my present condition, for fear of having my men completely demoralized.[22]

By early September, McCulloch was back in northwest Arkansas, organizing, training and resupplying his men and haggling with Richmond as well as with the state government in Little Rock for more men and arms. Just as he had planned, Sterling Price marched his State Guard north and captured Lexington on the Missouri River. Just as McCulloch had predicted, Price was only able to hold the town just over a week before a force under the Federal department commander, General John C. Fremont, forced him to retreat.

Back in northwest Arkansas, McCulloch's men were put in camps of instruction and also began to enjoy the bounty of countryside that fall. Autumn in the Ozarks can be a glorious time, and Captain John Good of Texas wrote that "[w]e fare abundantly here. Flour, bacon, coffee, sugar, beans, salt, soap, candles, and fine peaches and apples" were available within half a mile of his camp.[23]

Major General Sterling Price, commander of the Missouri State Guard. Wounded near Elkhorn Tavern on March 7. *Courtesy of the Library of Congress.*

Toward the end of September, McCulloch began a move north toward Kansas, planning to spend a month "ravaging the Territory" and then return to winter quarters, but his plans were never realized. First, an epidemic of measles laid low most of his army, and then he was forced to turn east when General Fremont, with a new army of thirty-eight thousand men, drove Price out of Springfield and threatened McCulloch's base at Fayetteville. By the first of November, McCulloch was back in Arkansas and had established his headquarters at Cross Hollow, seventeen miles south of the Missouri line on the Telegraph Road. His cavalry scouts ranged north along Telegraph Road and reported a large body of Federal troops marching south out of Springfield. Prepared to give them a "warm reception," McCulloch and everybody else were puzzled when the troops fell back and General Fremont disappeared.

On November 15, McCulloch received word from his scouts that the Federals were falling back from Springfield to the railhead at Rolla. He immediately put his troops on the road and, three days later, took possession of Springfield for the second time. Since the Federals outnumbered him at least five to one even in retreat, he decided not to pursue. What McCulloch did not know was that, on the first of November, General George McClellan had been made head of the Federal army, and one of his first acts was to replace General Fremont, first with General David Hunter, who withdrew the army from Springfield, and then with General Henry W. Halleck.

McCulloch had no intention of staying in Springfield with winter coming on. He had also heard that some representatives of Governor Jackson, some Missouri newspapermen and other Missouri partisans were spreading unfavorable reports about him to the Confederate government in Richmond, and he decided to go there in person to set the record straight. Not surprisingly, one of the main players in the anti-McCulloch campaign was none other than Sterling Price himself, which put an even greater strain on their relationship.[24] The day after he arrived in Springfield, McCulloch sent the following message:

HEADQUARTERS,
Springfield, Mo., November 19, 1861.
Honorable J.P. BENJAMIN, Secretary of War:

SIR: I shall return to Arkansas, put my troops in winter quarters soon, and ask permission to come immediately to Richmond, so as to give the administration correct information regarding affairs in this region before it acts on matters here. The Federals left [eight] days since with 30,000 men, quarreled among themselves, and greatly injured their cause by taking Negroes belonging to Union men. General Lane went to Kansas, General Hunter to Sedalia, and General Sigel to Rolla.

I have the honor to be, with respect, your obedient servant,
Ben. MCCULLOCH,
Brigadier-General, Commanding.[25]

By the first of December, McCulloch had his army back in Arkansas. He put most of his infantry into winter quarters in and around the Fayetteville area, while his mounted troops would winter in the Arkansas River Valley northeast of Van Buren along Frog Bayou, where the winter was somewhat milder and there was forage for the animals. Then, leaving Colonel James McIntosh in command, McCulloch and his adjutant, Frank C. Armstrong, left for the one-thousand-mile trip to the Confederate capital.[26] However, if Ben McCulloch thought, now that winter had come, that he would have plenty of time to clear things up in Richmond and then come back to plan his own spring offensive, he was badly mistaken.

Chapter 5

The Army of the Southwest

As Christmas approached in St. Louis, Major General Henry W. Halleck struggled to bring some order out of the chaos of Fremont's old department. When he took command on November 9, 1861, Halleck inherited a rather varied group of subordinates. East of the Mississippi, there was Ulysses S. Grant, district commander at Cairo, Illinois, with his slightly scruffy look and the persistent rumors of a drinking problem. A West Pointer but a mere captain in the old army, Brigadier General Grant was now responsible for the critical area of western Kentucky, including the Tennessee and Cumberland Rivers.

The division commanders under Grant certainly formed an odd couple. John A. McClernand was an Illinois politician appointed a general because of his connections to the Lincoln administration. With little military experience but large political ambitions, McClernand would bear watching closely. Grant's other division commander, stationed at Paducah, was McClernand's polar opposite. With thirty-six years in the army, Charles Ferguson Smith was a professional soldier right off a recruiting poster. Having graduated from West Point in 1825, he was an instructor there when both Halleck and Grant were cadets. Due to the quirks of promotions early in the war, however, Smith was now serving under his two former students. Where both McClernand and Grant would be looked on with suspicion by Halleck, Smith would be as solid as a rock.

Finally, there was the fleet. Here in the heartland, rivers were the superhighways of the Western Theater, and so Henry Halleck also inherited a "Brown Water" navy, commanded by Flag Officer Andrew H. Foote. Going to sea at age sixteen, Foote had spent thirty-nine years in the navy all over the world. Halleck's inland navy was in good hands.

On the west side of the river, other general officers commanded Halleck's troops, among them men such as Benjamin Prentiss, John Pope and William T. Sherman, who would later make their own marks, but for one man, the department commander had something else in mind.

Samuel R. Curtis was a West Pointer who had spent most of his life after the academy in the civilian world. He went back in the service during the war with Mexico but served as an administrator instead of a combat leader. Most recently, he had been a civil engineer and politician, being one of the first men from the new Republican Party to be elected to Congress. When the war began, he left his Congressional seat to accept the colonelcy of the Second Iowa Regiment. Long before the regiment saw any action, however, Curtis was promoted to brigadier general and transferred to Department Headquarters at St. Louis.

When Halleck arrived in November, Curtis was a great help in cleaning up the mess left by the previous commander, and now Halleck had a special job for him. Halleck was already planning an offensive for the spring, with one part of his force moving up the Tennessee and Cumberland Rivers and another moving down the Mississippi. Before those moves got underway, however, Halleck was determined to rid himself of the nuisances of Sterling Price and his Missouri State Guard. Even in their present weakened state, they were still capable of raising all sorts of havoc and tying down valuable resources that would be needed for the offensive. Samuel Curtis's assignment was to either destroy Price's forces or push him completely out of Missouri.

On Christmas Day 1861, Halleck issued a Special Order, and just a few weeks short of his fifty-seventh birthday, Samuel Curtis had his first combat command:

> SPECIAL ORDERS, {HDQRS. DEPARTMENT OF THE MISSOURI, Number 92.}
> Saint Louis, December 25, 1861.
>
> III. Brigadier General S.R. Curtis is assigned to the command of the Southwestern District of Missouri, including the country south of the Osage and west of the Meramec River.
>
> By order of Major-General Halleck: J.C. KELTON, Assistant Adjutant-General.[27]

By the next evening, Curtis had arrived at Rolla, the end of the railroad and his supply base, and introduced himself to a very surprised and angry Brigadier General Franz Sigel. Only two days earlier, Sigel had received orders to take command of all the forces in the Rolla area. Compounding matters was the fact that Curtis had moved so quickly to his new command that he arrived before the official notification from headquarters, causing some reluctance on Sigel's part to obey. A few days later, Curtis reported on the encounter:

> SAML. R. CURTIS, Brigadier-General.
> HEADQUARTERS SOUTHWESTERN DISTRICT, Rolla, December 29, 1861.
> Captain J.C. KELTON, Assistant Adjutant-General, Saint Louis, Mo.:
>
> CAPTAIN:
> I arrived here 8 p.m. Thursday night and immediately rode to the camp of Brigadier-General Sigel, about 3 miles from town. I communicated to him the wishes of the major-general in regard to moving the cavalry forthwith, and requested him to order immediate preparation for the movements. The general not having received the order placing me in command of the district and I not having assumed command (wishing to treat the general with all possible courtesy by conferring with him beforehand), it was with some expressions of doubt as to my rank and authority that he finally issued the order to the cavalry to report when they could move. Yesterday morning your telegraphic copy of Order 92 was received by General Sigel, and at his request I gave him the date of my commission and showed him our relative position in the Army Registers.[28]

What would have simply been a squabble between officers about seniority and wounded pride under normal circumstances soon developed into a full-blown political incident, with repercussions all the way to the White House.

Franz Sigel was born in 1824 in the town of Sinsheim in what was then the Grand Duchy of Baden. He graduated from the Military Academy at Karlsruhe and was involved in the unsuccessful revolution in Germany beginning in 1848. By 1852, Sigel had immigrated to the United States and, at the beginning of the war, was living in St. Louis, teaching at the Deutsches Institut and serving as a district superintendent in the public school system. He was also one of the most influential voices in the large St. Louis German immigrant community.[29]

Sigel firmly believed that he should lead the coming campaign and took Curtis's appointment as department commander as part of a plot by Henry Halleck to remove him from command. A large number of the troops at Rolla were also German immigrants and were fiercely loyal to Sigel—"I fights mit Sigel" was their slogan—so the quarrel quickly became a political crisis when Sigel resigned in protest. For the first few weeks of the new year, speeches and newspaper articles from all over the North came to Sigel's defense, and even President Lincoln was forced to consider some way to appease the large German community whose support he desperately needed. Finally, letters were exchanged and apologies given, and Sigel agreed to withdraw his resignation and serve under Curtis. Sigel was appointed Curtis's second in command, and operationally, he would directly command the two divisions made up mainly of German immigrants—roughly half the army. Even though the crisis seemed to be over, neither side really trusted the other. Sigel still considered Henry Halleck "a trickster," and both Halleck and Curtis knew that they would have to keep General Sigel on as short a leash as possible.[30]

While all of this was going on, Sterling Price had left his camps on the Osage River near Osceola and moved south to Springfield, arriving there on December 22. His men were now building shelters and settling into what they hoped would be winter quarters. Price was also beginning the process of transferring his units from the State Guard into regular Confederate service, now that Governor Jackson and the pro-Southern "government in exile" had finally adopted an Ordinance of Secession on October 31.[31]

When the reports of Price's movement into Springfield were first received, the thought was that he was retreating on farther south, and Halleck ordered Curtis to send a cavalry force to harass him (this was the cavalry mentioned in his report dated December 29 quoted earlier). Colonel Eugene Carr took the column but soon reported that Price and his Missouri State Guard were not retreating but rather settling in to stay. Henry Halleck, normally the most deliberate of commanders, was anxious to move but had not received permission from Washington. Finally, in response to a rumor that later proved to be false, Halleck ordered Curtis forward on January 13 on his own responsibility.

Over the next two weeks, Curtis brought his army sixty-three miles from Rolla southeast to Lebanon, Missouri, where Carr and the cavalry were waiting. The army marched along what was called Telegraph Road, which was the main route into Springfield and down into Arkansas. The army had hacked the road out of the Ozark wilderness almost twenty-five years earlier, and in addition to becoming the supply route for frontier forts, it also became part of the "Trail of Tears." Settlement along it was sparse until the Butterfield Stage Line improved it somewhat and began using it for its run from St. Louis to Fort Smith in 1858. Two years later, a telegraph line was strung along it, providing its current name.

Telegraph Road (or Wire Road, as it was sometimes called) might have been almost adequate for a Butterfield stagecoach every day or so, but for the thousands of men, animals and vehicles of Curtis's army, it was a nightmare. On a good day, it would have been a chore, but now, with the temperature near freezing, it began to rain. Soon the men and the baggage were soaked, and the freezing and thawing turned the road to mush. One soldier described the trek down to Lebanon simply as "mud without mercy."[32]

At Lebanon, Colonel Jefferson C. Davis's division joined the army, having marched down from Sedalia, and Curtis began to put the Army of the Southwest into its final form. To attempt to forestall any more trouble, he placed the mainly immigrant units into two divisions under their own officers, the First Division under Colonel Peter Osterhaus, a German, and the Second Division under Brigadier General Alexander S. Asboth, a Hungarian, with Sigel in overall command. In addition to command of the army as a whole, Curtis had under his direct command the Third Division under Colonel Jefferson C. Davis (Indiana and Illinois men) and the Fourth Division under Colonel Eugene A. Carr (Iowa, Illinois and Missouri men). At Lebanon, the army's troop strength came to just over twelve thousand men and fifty pieces of artillery.[33]

Everybody in the Federal Army of the Southwest knew that the survival of the army in the wilds of the Ozark Mountains would depend on its supply line from the railhead at Rolla, and every

Colonel Jefferson C. Davis, commander of the Federal Third Division. Davis and his division reinforced Colonel Peter Osterhaus north of Leetown on March 7. *Courtesy of the Library of Congress.*

Captain Phillip H. Sheridan (shown here as a brigadier general), quartermaster general of the Federal Army of the Southwest. *Courtesy of the Library of Congress.*

step they made farther south made that line longer. Keeping up with the army's needs would require an immense effort, and Halleck thought that he had found just the man to be Curtis's quartermaster. It would be Captain Phillip H. Sheridan's job to keep Curtis's army alive and fighting. An 1853 West Point graduate, Phil Sheridan would prove to be a highly efficient if sometimes prickly junior officer who was destined for great things. Less than a year after he served as a captain on Curtis's staff, Sheridan would be a major general.

While Curtis organized his army at Lebanon, Sterling Price sat fifty miles away in Springfield and watched the developments with dismay. Even in the dead of winter, Curtis gave every indication of preparing to advance. Price didn't want to have to retreat again in this weather, but with barely seven thousand effectives, he stood little chance of being able to hold Springfield if Curtis made a determined effort. Had he known the Union assessment of his forces, it would not have cheered him. On January 2, Colonel Frederick Steele sent this report: "Two of my spies just in from Springfield humbugged Price completely; went through all his camps safely; saw everything…At present he has no discipline, no roll-calls, no sentinels, nor picket to prevent passing in and out of Springfield. Rains [Brigadier General James S. Rains] drunk all the time. Price also drinking too much."[34]

As soon as he became aware of Curtis's army, Price began bombarding McCulloch in Arkansas with pleas for reinforcement. McCulloch being in Richmond, these request came to his second in command, the newly promoted Brigadier General James McIntosh, who had no intention of marching the Confederate forces out of their winter quarters on his own initiative. Knowing that he must retreat, Price still waited until almost the last minute.

Brigadier General Samuel R. Curtis, commander of the Federal Army of the Southwest. *Courtesy of the Library of Congress.*

On February 10, Samuel Curtis and the Army of the Southwest marched out of Lebanon, Missouri, on Henry Halleck's second offensive in just over a week. Eight days earlier, Halleck had unleashed Ulysses S. Grant and an army that would eventually grow to more than twenty-five thousand on the Confederate forts on the Tennessee and Cumberland Rivers. Now he was sending Curtis to rid Missouri of Sterling Price and his State Guard. The stakes were high for Henry Halleck. Defeat of either of these armies would deal perhaps a fatal blow to his carefully constructed career. As he had told Grant, he now told Curtis: failure was not an option.[35]

The fickle winter weather had turned mild and dry, and by February 12, Curtis was only eight miles out of Springfield. Price sent some cavalry out to make a demonstration to delay the Yankees, and then, in the night, he and his men slipped out of town. McCulloch and his Confederates had not come to him. Now, although he didn't know it quite yet, he was on his way to join them. So began Price's one-hundred-mile running fight into the Boston Mountains of northwest Arkansas.

Chapter 6

Price's Retreat

Sterling Price's delaying action had the intended effect. Colonel Elijah Gates had taken his First Missouri Cavalry out just after dark and skirmished with some Federal horsemen along Pierson's Creek, giving the rest of Price's army time to get on the road out of Springfield. The next morning, thinking that the previous night's raid could mean that Price had decided to defend Springfield, the Federals moved forward very deliberately. The advanced units met no resistance, however, and by midmorning, the Stars and Stripes flew over the courthouse in Springfield. The Missouri town had changed hands for the last time.

In its haste, Price's army left many things. About six hundred sick and wounded, as well as stragglers, were still in town, along with a fair amount of military stores and rations that they had not been able to move. Most of the civilian population had fled also, and the town was in shambles. Federal units quickly fell on the commissary stores, and soon it was common to see soldiers carrying hams or sides of bacon on their bayonets. General Curtis moved into the same house that Price had used as a headquarters and found some of Price's correspondence that he had left behind. The men found whatever lodgings they could, with one newspaper correspondent traveling with the army describing his accommodations that night as having "the comfort of a small parlor bed room, and the elegance of a hog pen."[36]

All day on February 13 and into the night, the Federal army rested in Springfield and feasted on captured Confederate provisions, while the generals planned their next move. It was yet to be seen whether Price would retreat farther or stand and fight. There was also the question of whether McCulloch would come north out of Arkansas and reinforce him. For Curtis, however, there was never any question that he would continue to pursue Price until he was destroyed or was pushed out of Missouri.

At the staff meeting that evening in Curtis's quarters, General Sigel was quick to offer a plan that was somewhat risky yet offered the possibility of dealing with Price once and for all. Sigel proposed that Curtis take about half the army and follow Price down Telegraph Road while he, with the rest of the troops, would march on a smaller road a few miles to the west and try to get in Price's rear and cut him off at the town of McDowell, about twenty miles north of the Arkansas line. It meant dividing the army and counting on Sigel to force his men to march the extra ten miles or so quickly enough. It also counted on Price not being in any hurry to withdraw farther south or to turn and attack Curtis while Sigel was too far to the west to reinforce him—a lot of "ifs."

Sigel's plan, in fact, sounded a lot like the one that, six months earlier, had brought Nathaniel Lyon and the Federal army to grief at Wilson's Creek, but the Federal commander decided to try it. A few days later, Curtis would get a message from Henry Halleck warning him against letting Sigel talk him into dividing his forces, just as he was about to do. By then, however, Sigel's plan had failed for reasons no one could have foreseen.[37]

On the morning of February 14, the Federal army set off after Price and his men. The land was covered in a thin layer of snow and ice from a storm the night before, but the Yankees had been fairly comfortable in Springfield. Price and his Missourians, however, had spent a miserable night camped in the open around McCullah's Spring. They, too, were on the move that morning but would only fall back to the Crane Creek Valley and go into camp. Price was not sure what the Yankees were up to and planned to spend a few days in this nice little valley waiting for their next move. The answer wouldn't be long in coming.

While Price only moved his men about eight miles back to Crane Creek, Curtis advanced all the way to Price's old camp at McCullah's Spring. Scouting on ahead of the main body late in the afternoon, Colonel Calvin Ellis and his First Missouri Cavalry (Union) made contact with Colonel Henry Little's First Missouri Brigade (Confederate), serving as Price's rear guard. Being on a hill looking down at the enemy bedding down for the evening was too good an opportunity for Ellis to pass up, so he brought up Major William Bowen and his four small mountain howitzers, and they lobbed ten shells into the Confederate camp. Ellis then broke off the action, took thirty prisoners and withdrew back to McCullah's Spring, not knowing that he had just sabotaged Curtis and Sigel's plan.[38]

Colonel Ellis and Major Bowen's little bombardment did little actual damage, but it certainly got the attention of General Sterling Price. Expecting Curtis to advance slowly if at all in the dead of winter, Price was shocked to find enemy cavalry and artillery already at the edge of his camps. Had he known that it was just a small incident by some of Curtis's forward scouts, things might have been different, but Price decided to take no chances. From then on it became a race for Arkansas.

Because the Yankees seemed so close, Price put his supply wagons out in front of the army and got them moving right away. Even so, it took all night for them to clear the camp so that the troops could get on the road south. Price's supply train was made up of every sort of rolling vehicle imaginable and took hours to pass. According to one Southern soldier, "[E]very species of wheel vehicle, from the jolting old ox-cart to the most fantastically painted stage coach rolled along the road."[39]

The shelling of the Confederate camp by a few small artillery pieces was enough to upset Curtis's plan. He had not meant to disturb the Confederates until Sigel could get in position at McDowell, but now they were off and running. Curtis angrily reprimanded Colonel Ellis, but it was too late. Early the next morning, Curtis put his army on the road and took up the chase. Sigel, meanwhile, was taking his time on his westerly route, just as Curtis had feared. When he finally arrived at McDowell's on February 16, Sigel found that he had not only missed the Confederates but that Curtis and the rest of the Federal army were ahead of him, too.

As the Confederates approached the Arkansas line, south of Keetsville, they came to a section of Telegraph Road that ran through a steep valley for about eight miles. Back in November, when there was the fear that General Fremont might invade, McCulloch's men had cut down trees to block this area that had become known locally as Cross Timbers Hollow. Since then, a narrow lane had been cleared through the fallen trees for wagon traffic, but it was still the perfect choke point for a delaying action. Henry Little's First Missouri Brigade (Confederate) was still the rear guard, and he dropped off Colonel Elijah Gates's First Missouri Cavalry and two of Captain Churchill Clark's guns to ambush the Federal pursuit. It turned out to be an all-Missouri affair as soon as Colonel Calvin Ellis's loyal First Missouri Cavalry arrived.

Clark's guns forced Ellis's riders to stop and deploy, but then the Rebels packed up and disappeared down the road. Tired of the cat-and-mouse game that had been going on for the last two days, Ellis remounted his men and set off after them at a gallop, catching Gates and his men around the bend and piling into them before the Rebels could deploy again. For a few minutes, loyal and Rebel Missourians thrashed around at the rear of the Confederate column until Colonel Little countermarched some of his infantry and drove the Yankees off. That night, Curtis's army camped in the edge of Missouri, while Price trudged on into Arkansas.

By now, the Confederates were exhausted. Few had gotten more than a couple of hours of sleep at a time since they had left Springfield, and all had marched over sixty miles in freezing temperatures. Not everybody made it. One Missouri Guardsman named McDaniel remembered waking up one morning with his clothes frozen on him and his feet swollen. When his commander came by, he said, "Oh God, Colonel, shoot me if you will, but don't tell me to fall in. I'm nearly dead and can't walk for the life of me."[40] He was lucky and got to ride on an artillery caisson that day, but many others simply fell out along the road to be picked up by the following Federals or to freeze in the woods. At one point, Curtis reported to headquarters in St. Louis that he was finding "more straggling prisoners than I know what to do with."[41]

Finally, as they crossed into Arkansas, the weary Missourians began to see some of McCulloch's troops who had come to meet them—men from Colonel Louis Hebert's brigade who were wintering in the area. Colonel Hebert had only received word that morning that Price and his army were coming, and as his men hurried north up Telegraph Road to meet them, they witnessed a scene that one said "beggared description" when they encountered Price's wagon train streaming south toward Fayetteville. Added to the army train were many private carriages and wagons filled with civilians fleeing the dreaded Yankee invasion.[42]

As Hebert's fresh Arkansas and Louisiana troops took up the rear guard, Price's worn-out men trudged past a tavern with giant elk antlers on the roof and on down Telegraph Road into the valley of Little Sugar Creek.[43] There they collapsed and had a decent supper and night's sleep for the first time in almost four days.[44]

The next morning, February 17, Hebert's men, who had also fallen back into the Little Sugar Creek Valley, half expected to see the Yankees on the bluffs that lined the north bank of the stream, but no one was there. Curtis had started early that morning, marching across the Arkansas line with flags flying and bands playing, but his advanced unit, still the First Missouri Cavalry under Colonel Ellis, would not arrive at Little Sugar Creek until just after noon. By then, most of Price's army was gone, but Ellis could still see

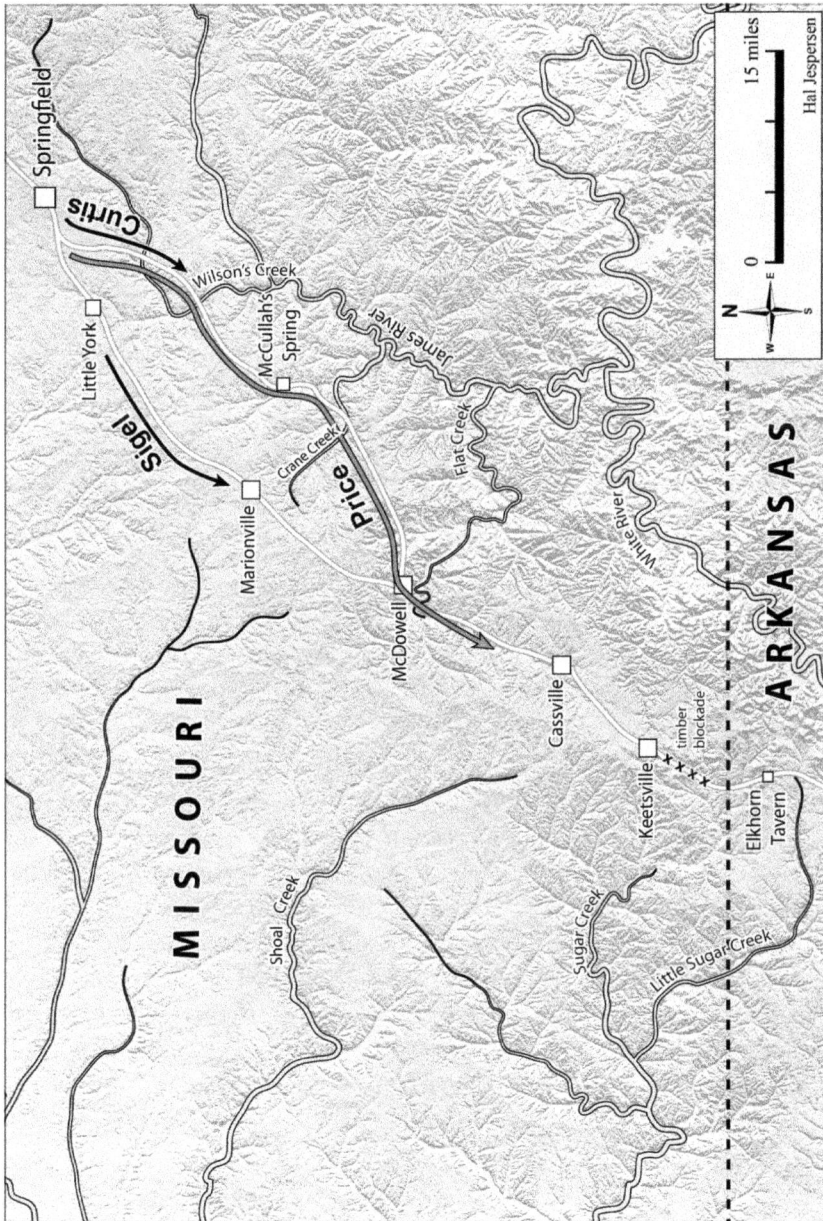

Price's retreat from Springfield to Little Sugar Creek, February 13–17. *Courtesy of Hal Jespersen.*

Dunagin's Farm, looking south toward the Confederates' position, modern view. *Author's collection.*

the rear guard across the valley. He sent word for Curtis to come up, but by the time the commander got there, the Rebels had disappeared behind the opposite ridgeline.

Louis Hebert thought that the Federals would be cautious crossing Little Sugar Creek in case he and his men might be waiting in ambush, so he was surprised to learn, not long after he had marched his men away, that the Yankees had thrown cavalry and artillery across the creek and were coming after him. He sent a rider on ahead after Colonel Henry Little, who was still watching the rear of Price's column, asking that he countermarch his brigade and come back to help. While he waited, Hebert faced his three regiments about and took up a blocking position on Telegraph Road along the south edge of a field owned by a local farmer named James Dunagin. Little's men soon arrived, and the Missourians took up positions on the west side of the road, with Hebert's Louisiana and Arkansas men on the east.

Not long after the Confederates were in position, Colonel Ellis came over the hill leading the Federal cavalry. Expecting a running fight like those he had seen for the last few days, Ellis led his men down the road at full speed and right into Hebert's position. Ellis realized his mistake when Captain Churchill Clark's battery fired its first salvo straight down the road, emptying a few saddles and bringing Ellis's charge to a halt. After a few minutes of hand-to-hand struggle, the Federal troops fell back into the timber on the north side of Dunagin's field, Curtis sent reinforcements forward and, as one Louisiana soldier put it, "For nearly an hour, a desperate fight ensued in which artillery was freely used on both sides…The dash of the Federal Cavalry was so impetuous that they became intermingled with our troops, and there was free use of sabers and small arms."[45]

In the end, the Confederates withdrew safely to the south, and the Federals were content to let them go. So ended the Battle of Dunagin's Farm (sometimes called the Battle of Little Sugar Creek), the first Civil War engagement fought on Arkansas soil.

Chapter 7

The End of the Chase

S itting in his office at St. Louis on the morning of Tuesday, February 18, Major General Henry W. Halleck should have been a happy man. Against most accepted military wisdom, he had launched two different offensives—headed in opposite directions—in the middle of winter, and both had been very successful. To the east, Brigadier General Ulysses S. Grant had an army of almost twenty-five thousand in Tennessee, having taken both Fort Henry and Fort Donelson, gained control of the Tennessee and the Cumberland Rivers and captured twelve to fifteen thousand prisoners. To the southwest, Brigadier General Samuel Curtis's army of just over ten thousand sat on Little Sugar Creek, eight miles into Arkansas, having pushed Sterling Price's State Guard completely out of Missouri.[46]

As successful as these two operations had been, no one, least of all Samuel Curtis, thought that the issue had been decided. Curtis had certainly accomplished his mission—to rid Missouri of Sterling Price—but now he sat at the end of a thin supply line almost two hundred miles long with no hope of reinforcement, facing a combined Confederate army that now outnumbered him by almost seven thousand men.

General Grant had forced Confederate general Albert Sidney Johnston to abandon his entire defensive line and fall back almost two hundred miles. Grant was, for now at least, the unchallenged master of Middle Tennessee and its two vital rivers. Samuel Curtis, on the other hand, sat only a few miles from a numerically superior and belligerent enemy army that he had helped create by driving Price into the somewhat reluctant arms of Ben McCulloch's better armed and much more capable Confederate Army of the West. Even so, Curtis had no intention of falling back into Missouri. If the Confederates turned and came after him—as he fully expected they would—he would do his best to be ready.

The Federal army spent the night of the seventeenth in the Little Sugar Creek Valley, while Price's Missourians trudged on a few miles south to the large Confederate camp at Cross Hollow. Early the next morning, Curtis had scouts out searching the area to the west for opportunities to outflank the Confederate position, and Brigadier General Alexander Asboth, with some mounted troops, was sent about ten miles to the west to the small town of Bentonville. Asboth was a Hungarian officer who had come to America in 1851, after a failed revolution in Hungry, and was now commanding a division in Franz Sigel's part of General Curtis's army. Asboth and his men rode into Bentonville at about noon, captured about thirty prisoners, hauled down the regimental flag of the Seventeenth Arkansas from atop the courthouse and were back to Little Sugar Creek by sundown.[47] As a result of the reconnaissance, Curtis was prepared to move the army to the west the next day, but that turned out to be unnecessary.

While the Federals were reconnoitering to the west on the eighteenth, General Ben McCulloch arrived at the Confederate camp at Cross Hollow to a huge welcome by his men. McCulloch then conferred with Price, and as usual, the two generals disagreed. Price was all for standing and fighting where he was, but McCulloch believed that they should withdraw farther south. As the Confederates settled in for the second night, the weather turned colder, and a freezing rain began to fall. W.L. Grammage, surgeon of the Fourth Arkansas, recalled that "the entire night was pretty well divided between unavailable efforts to keep my feet from freezing and my body from floating in the thawing sleet."[48]

During the night, a report of Asboth's raid on Bentonville came in that finally brought General Price around to McCulloch's view that they should fall back, since it seemed that the enemy was trying to get around their left flank. On the morning of February 19, the Confederates continued the march on to the south. General Curtis soon learned that the Confederates were withdrawing and changed his plans for a flanking movement. Instead, he advanced straight ahead down Telegraph Road. The retreating Confederates had done their best to burn the camp as they left, but many of the buildings at Cross Hollow were still standing and were occupied by the Federals that night.

Fayetteville, the seat of Washington County, was the largest town in the area and the commercial and cultural hub of northwest Arkansas. In the fall of

1860, it had a population of about two thousand, with two female seminaries; Arkansas College, a men's school with almost two hundred students; a large stable complex operated by Overland Mail Company; a large steam-powered mill capable of producing ten thousand pounds of flour per day; and several other local businesses. At the beginning of the war, Fayetteville was, by all accounts, a beautiful and prosperous town. Since the fall of 1861, however, Fayetteville had been occupied by Ben McCulloch's Confederate forces.

Reverend William Baxter, a local minister and educator and the president of Arkansas College, gave this description of Fayetteville after General McCulloch fell back into northwest Arkansas following the Battle of Wilson's Creek:

> Our town then became a military post. The Pelican Rifles and Iberville Grays of the 3rd Louisiana Infantry were quartered in the College building; the Female Seminary was used as an arsenal; and the stables of the Overland Mail Company were seized for the use of the Government. Soon we had a crowd of commissaries and quarter-masters with their employees; next a flood of Confederate money. Fugitive Missourians found our town a very paradise for horse dealers…Depots for beef and pork were established and were rapidly filling; food for a large army was collected; mills were pressed for the military service.[49]

The town of Fayetteville was the next stop for Price's Missouri army on its way south.

Early on the morning of February 19, Price's Missouri Guard and McCulloch's Confederates left Cross Hollow, firing as much of the camp as they could, and marched south in miserable weather. One of the Louisiana soldiers later remembered:

> On Tuesday morning [sic], very early, our army began to retreat in the midst of a bitter cold storm of sleet and snow. The road was a mass of solid ice, slippery and hard as a rock…All day long the weary march continued, while the beards of the men became white with their frozen breath, even the water in the canteens turning into ice.[50]

That night, a trickle of men began to reach Fayetteville. By the next morning, the twentieth, it had become a flood.

General McCulloch never intended to make a stand in Fayetteville. He meant to fall back to the winter camps south of the town near Strickler's

Station. Unfortunately, there was a huge cache of food and materials in Fayetteville that the Confederates, burdened as they already were, simply could not remove. McCulloch, therefore, made the decision to open the military storehouses to everyone—military and civilian alike—rather than letting it fall into Federal hands. When the exhausted and half-starved Missourians arrived to find the storehouse doors wide open, it was like Christmas in February, and the results were as predictable as they were destructive. Very soon, the rampaging soldiers ceased to make the distinction between army warehouses and the civilian stores and houses nearby, and the looting became general.

Many of the Confederate officers were appalled at what was happening but were powerless to stop it. One said that it was "one of the most disgraceful scenes that I ever saw." Another estimated that almost half a million pounds of pork was either carried off by the soldiers or burned in bonfires to keep themselves warm. Most of the army camped just to the south, but many of the officers spent one last night in town. The next morning, expecting the Federals to arrive any time, the remainder of the Confederates beat a hasty retreat, but then some cavalry returned and set fire to several of the buildings used by the military. The local people had little equipment to fight the fires, and soon much of the town was in flames.[51]

All through that day and into the next, the Southern soldiers moved south into the Boston Mountains until they came to the Confederate camps at Strickler's Station. The Missouri men's long retreat was finally over. Back in Fayetteville, the townspeople spent most of February 21 fighting the fires, with mixed results. Some private homes and businesses were saved, but others perished. A few large explosions rocked the building formerly occupied by the Fayetteville Female Institute (headed by T.B. Van Horne), which had been used as a factory for making cartridges and shells. This only spread the flames further and faster. As one Fayetteville resident later said, "The few citizens who remained could do little toward arresting the progress of fires in so many different places at the same time, and when night fell, a great portion of our town was a smoldering ruin."[52]

General Curtis, still camped at Cross Hollow, soon learned from loyal Union men in the area that the Confederates had fallen back south of Fayetteville. On Sunday morning, February 23, he sent General Asboth with about 1,200 troops down Telegraph Road to conduct a reconnaissance in force as far as Fayetteville. The men had no trouble brushing aside the few Confederate pickets still left and rode into town just before noon, to the delight of the many Union sympathizers there. A long-hidden Union flag

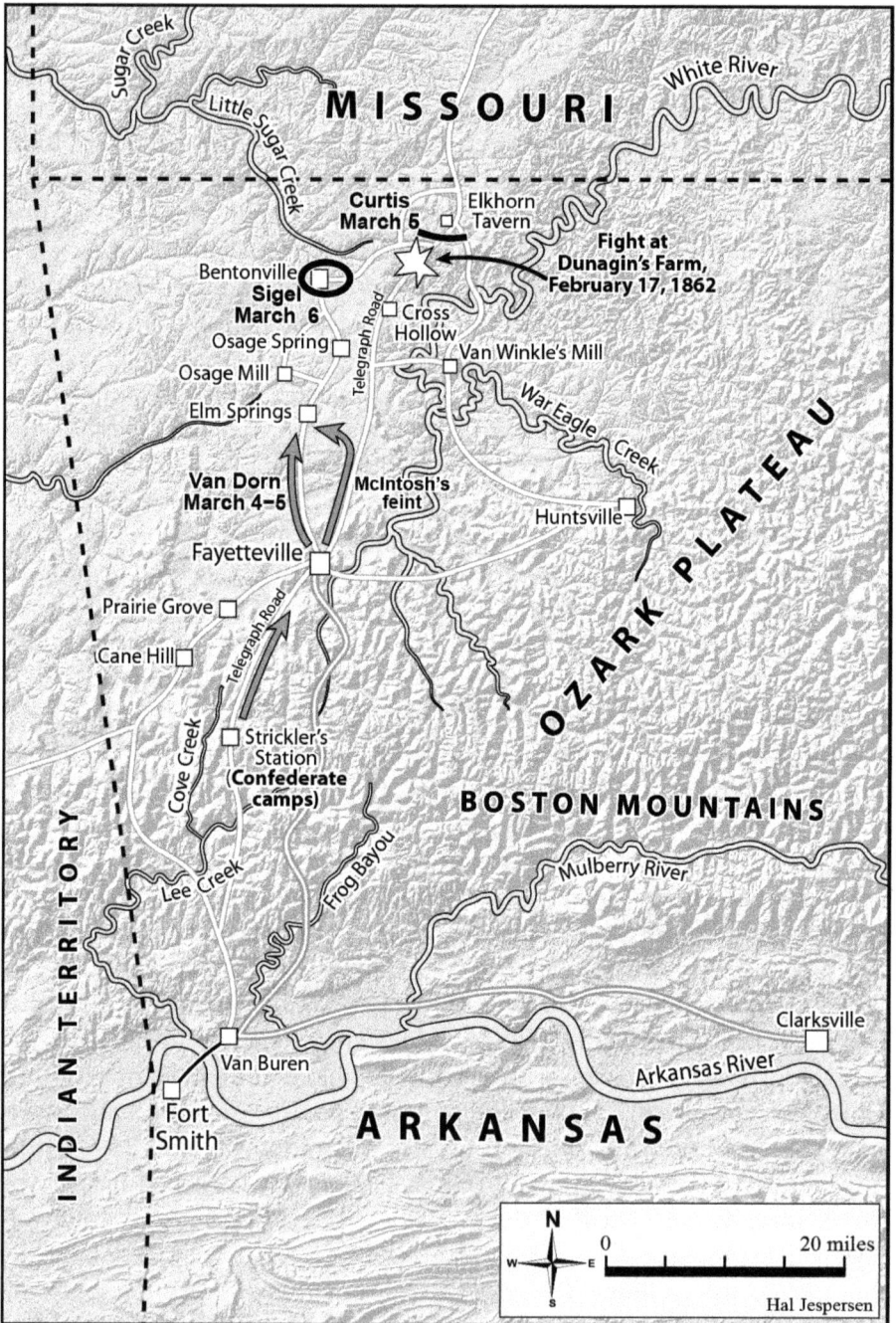

Price's retreat from Cross Hollow to the Confederate camps in the Boston Mountains (February 19–22) and Van Dorn's advance on Bentonville (March 4–6). *Courtesy of Hal Jespersen.*

was produced and soon flew over the courthouse. General Asboth reported his success to General Curtis and stated that, with two more regiments, he could hold the town.[53] The loyal Union men in Fayetteville now thought that they were under the protection to the Federal army, but it was not to be.

As badly as the loyalists in Fayetteville wanted them to stay, Asboth and his men were ordered to fall back to Cross Hollow only two days later. Curtis was well aware that he was leaving the loyal citizens in Fayetteville in a dangerous situation, since their welcoming of the Federal troops would not be forgotten when the Confederates came back to town, but he felt that it was too exposed a position. Curtis had decided to consolidate his forces nearer to Little Sugar Creek and let the Confederates make the next move.

During the last few days of February, Samuel Curtis set his army up to cover the two routes available to the Confederates when they decided to come north. Curtis, with Colonel Eugene Carr's division, sat on Telegraph Road at Cross Hollow. Behind him about ten miles, Colonel Jefferson Davis and his division settled in on the north bank of Little Sugar Creek atop the bluffs overlooking the stream. This would be Curtis's fallback position when the time came.

To guard the Elm Springs Road about six miles to the west, the other possible avenue of advance for the Confederates, Curtis sent General Sigel with his two divisions under General Asboth and Colonel Osterhaus to the area around Bentonville and McKissick's Creek. Farther out on each end of the line, smaller units operated two mills—Blackburn's Mill on the east and Osage Mill on the west—grinding flour and cornmeal for the army. Samuel Curtis's army may have been the only Civil War army to march into battle carrying fifty hand-operated portable grinding mills, but regular working mills like Blackburn's on War Eagle Creek were much preferred, and when the Federals found them undamaged by the Confederates, they used them and guarded them well. It was much easier to use local mills to grind local wheat and corn into flour and meal than to haul it in from Missouri.[54]

By the first of March, Samuel Curtis had chosen his ground. He covered the two likely approaches that the enemy would use and was actively patrolling in front of his line. His men were supplementing their supplies with grain and fodder available locally, and he was preparing a fallback position on Little Sugar Creek, where he expected to make the main fight when the time came. He had pushed Price out of Missouri and had no intention of giving up his foothold in northwest Arkansas. He knew that Price and McCulloch, as well as their new commander, Earl Van Dorn, could not let the situation stand as it was. They would be coming. It was just a matter of time.

Chapter 8

The Confederates Advance

February 22, the day when Price and his Missourians finally reached the winter camp in the Boston Mountains, also happened to be the day when Major General Earl Van Dorn, the new department commander, learned that Price was not still in Springfield. Van Dorn had been busy planning a spring offensive toward St. Louis from his headquarters at Pocahontas, but Price's retreat and the presence of a Federal army in northwest Arkansas changed his plans. Van Dorn immediately decided to go and take command of Price and McCulloch's troops personally. He still held out hope for his spring offensive, and if Curtis's army could be defeated, the road to St. Louis would still be open, just from a slightly different direction. Within two days, Van Dorn was on his way west, accompanied only by his chief of staff, Colonel Dabney H. Maury; his aide and nephew, Lieutenant Clement Sulivane; and his personal servant, Milton.[55]

Van Dorn and his group pushed hard, averaging more than fifty miles per day, and by the time they reached Van Buren on March 1, the general was suffering from chills and fever, having fallen in the Little Red River during their crossing, as well as being exposed to freezing winds during the two-hundred-mile trip.[56] At Van Buren, however, General Van Dorn found a telegram waiting for him from General McCulloch that he found very encouraging:

The Civil War Fight for the Ozarks

HEADQUARTERS MCCULLOCH'S DIVISION, March 1, 1862.

General VAN DORN:

SIR: I have ordered the command to be ready to march as soon as you arrive, with six days' cooked rations, and will notify General Price to be ready also. We await your arrival anxiously. We now have force enough to whip the enemy.

Your obedient servant, BEN. MCCULLOCH, Brigadier-General.

The next day, Earl Van Dorn and his little group struggled on north into the Boston Mountains and arrived at General Price's headquarters on Cove Creek late that Sunday afternoon, March 2. Price fed them what Maury remembered as a "glorious supper" and made them comfortable for the night in a large tent with beds, blankets and buffalo robes. The next morning, to Maury's amazement, breakfast consisted of kidneys stewed in sherry, showing that Price, although driven from his state and into the Arkansas wilderness, was making the best of his circumstances.[57]

After retreating over one hundred miles in miserable winter weather with little sleep, food or protection from the elements, Price's Missouri men had spent the last week in the relative luxury of the Confederate camps around Strickler's Station and Cove Creek. The weather even moderated, and some of Price's Missourians received uniforms for the first time. They were made of homespun wool with wooden buttons and smelled strongly of sheep, but finally they were looking more like an army than a mob.[58]

During that week of relative calm and decent weather, McCulloch's cavalry was busy. Knowing that Curtis's supply line was long and vulnerable, McCulloch sent the Sixth Texas Cavalry under Major Lawrence Sullivan "Sul" Ross behind the Federal lines. Ross had served in the Texas Rangers and with Van Dorn on temporary duty with the U.S. Army in Texas and Indian Territory before the war, so both of his commanders knew him well. On February 25, Ross and his Texans appeared at Keetsville, Missouri, twenty-five miles behind the Federal lines. They drove off the small garrison, burned several wagons and made off with about sixty horses and mules. On their way back, they circled to the east and came close enough to War Eagle Creek to cause Colonel Grenville Dodge, whose Fourth Iowa Regiment was there operating Blackburn's Mill, to abandon the place and fall back closer to Little Sugar Creek.[59]

The Confederate cavalry had also been keeping close tabs on the Federal army, so when General Van Dorn met with Price and McCulloch the next day (March 3), they were able to give him a very good picture of Curtis's deployment. It was obvious that the best case for the Confederates would be to catch the Federal army while it was still divided, so Van Dorn decided to march immediately on Franz Sigel's two divisions camped in and around Bentonville. If they could move fast enough and bring all of their forces to bear on Sigel, they would outnumber him almost three to one. They could then turn on Curtis with a similar advantage. Speed and deception was the key. They would have to march back north to Fayetteville and then out along Elm Springs Road to Bentonville—about thirty-eight miles—without being discovered.

Van Dorn, a cavalryman at heart, would conduct this operation like he was still back in Texas fighting Indians. The army would have to travel light, so orders were given that all the tents and camp equipment be left behind. The men would march with their rifle, forty rounds in their cartridge boxes, one blanket and three days' rations in their knapsacks. This last item was somewhat dubious at best, since most Civil War soldiers could easily eat in one day all the rations a small knapsack would hold. Making a knapsack full of food last three days—much less six, as General McCulloch had initially stated—meant short rations for sure. A supply train with additional ammunition and rations would follow the army, but until its arrival, the army would have to live off the land and captured enemy resources. As there was no time to waste, they would march out the next morning.

In order to gather as much manpower as he could, McCulloch had earlier issued a call for "emergency men" to come forward for a short period to help, and some of those units were just now arriving. Being just formed and practically unarmed, most would not be much of a factor in the coming battle.[60] Brigadier General Albert Pike's Creek and Cherokee troops were another matter. They were a few miles away to the west, so orders were sent for Pike to bring his men over from Indian Territory and join the army on the march.[61]

The next morning (March 4), the army moved out to the north in a late winter snowstorm. The good weather of the past week had changed again. One of the men of the Third Louisiana remembered it this way: "The first day's march was toward Fayetteville. The snow and sleet were blinding and the roads in an awful condition. We halted for the night, but, of course, anything like sleep was out of the question…The second day, the weather was somewhat better and the sun shone a little."[62]

Unknown to Van Dorn, on this first day his plan was already in jeopardy. Samuel Curtis had gotten nervous about his army's spread-out deployment, as well as the dwindling amount of fodder to be found where they were, and on March 3, he had told Sigel to fall back to the position on Little Sugar Creek. Since there had not yet been any indication that the Confederates were on the move, Sigel felt no need to rush and was taking his time, as usual. This left Van Dorn a small window of opportunity, but time was running out.[63]

The next morning (March 5), Van Dorn's infantry, with Price leading off, started north from Fayetteville on the Elm Springs Road. Hoping to distract Curtis, he also sent Brigadier General James McIntosh with his mounted brigade north on Telegraph Road toward Curtis's position at Cross Hollow to make a demonstration. After getting Curtis's attention, they were then to turn west and rejoin the main column near Elm Springs.

The march north was grueling, especially on the infantry trudging through the snow and sleet and mud. A Third Louisiana soldier later wrote, "It seemed as if General Van Dorn imagined the men were made of cast-steel, with the strength and powers of endurance of a horse…Scarcely time was given the men to prepare food and snatch a little rest."[64]

It did not help matters that the general had taken ill shortly after leaving the camps and bounced along the road, snug in his ambulance, while the men marched.

While the Confederates advanced undetected north from Fayetteville, things were happening on the Federal side also. Just as the Rebels left their camps on the fourth, Colonel Eugene Carr at Cross Hollow sent Colonel William Vandever with about seven hundred men off through the same snowstorm to Huntsville, thirty-five miles to the east, to check on a report of Confederate troops in the area. In Sigel's camp near Bentonville, another group under Major Joseph Conrad was sent west to Maysville on the Indian Territory line. More critical, however, was that Sigel had also begun drawing in his pickets, presumably in preparation for the move to Little Sugar Creek ordered by Curtis the day before. As part of this move, the cavalry outpost at Elm Springs was brought in, leaving the road from Bentonville to Fayetteville unguarded as Van Dorn's army approached. It was just possible that the Confederates were about to get the break they needed.[65]

Chapter 9

The Affair at Bentonville

During the day of March 5, the Confederate advance was going about as well as could be expected. The main column of infantry was making slow but steady progress north on the Elm Springs Road, while General McIntosh and his mounted troops moved up Telegraph Road toward the Federal camp at Cross Hollow. As they approached the forward Federal outpost at a little village called Mud Town, McIntosh sent the Sixth Texas Cavalry forward to cause as much commotion as it could and then fall back toward Elm Springs. McIntosh then swung the rest of his troopers west to cut across country toward the town of Elm Springs.

The Sixth Texas, under Colonel Warren Stone, had the good fortune to come upon a Federal foraging party near Mud Town, which they captured, and then they fired on the Federal pickets in the town. Having served their purpose, they then fell back. General McIntosh and his men crossed the six or seven miles of broken country to the west and still reached Elm Springs long before the main column. Since Sigel had withdrawn his outpost the day before, they met no resistance. While they waited for the main body to arrive, McIntosh sent patrols north on both sides of the road to gather up any stray Federal pickets or stragglers.

Late in the afternoon, the infantry began to arrive, and Elm Springs proved to be a decent place to spend the night. This came at a good time, since the weather remained very cold, with intermittent snow showers. Dr. Washington L. Grammage, surgeon of the Fourth Arkansas, noted that "[t]he night of the 5th found us at Elm Springs, where I was fortunate enough to find a house to sleep in and a straw pile to spread my blanket upon."[66] Those who were not so lucky to find indoor lodgings were at least allowed to build large fires to keep warm. While the main body of the Confederates were getting some desperately needed rest, Colonel Elkanah Greer and his Third Texas Cavalry were carefully patrolling north on Elm Springs Road toward Bentonville, with specific orders not to alert the Federals to their presence, when their luck ran out.

On March 4, the day before the Confederates arrived, probably the person most alarmed by General Sigel's order to withdraw the outpost at Elm Springs was Colonel Frederick Schaefer, whose loyal Second Missouri Regiment was now left alone south of Sigel's main camp at McKissick's Creek. Schaefer and his men were at Osage Mill, just over two miles west of the Elm Springs/Bentonville Road. (There was a small settlement on that road called Osage Springs, and the two places are often confused.) Colonel Schaefer had no intention of leaving the vital road unguarded, so he extended his infantry picket line to the east to cover it. The line intersected the road about five miles north of Elm Springs.

Late in the afternoon, as Greer's Third Texas Cavalry worked its way carefully north, the failing light and blowing snow reduced the visibility to the point that the Texas troopers ran into Schaefer's outpost before they knew it. The loyal Missouri boys put up a stubborn fight until darkness forced both sides to retire. The Texas horsemen fell back to Elm Springs, and the Missouri men fell back to Osage Mills. The Confederates had been discovered.[67]

In fact, the Confederates' march north had been discovered even before the little skirmish north of Elm Springs. Not long after the Sixth Texas's demonstration at Mud Town, word of Van Dorn's march north had come to General Curtis at Cross hollow. A loyal man from Fayetteville came to the camp and told Curtis what he had seen as the Confederates had marched through town on their way north the day before. Later on that evening, one of Curtis's spies also reported in. He was a Missouri man who was actually riding with the Confederates, pretending to be a Southern sympathizer. Curtis was convinced by the two reports and sent two urgent messages to Sigel, telling him to fall back to Little Sugar Creek immediately, making a night march if necessary.

Curtis's two messages reached Sigel, but it was the report of Colonel Schaefer from Osage Mills that his men had actually encountered Rebel cavalry on the Elm Springs Road within five miles of Bentonville that caused Sigel to finally take the threat seriously. The German general called a staff meeting at 1:00 a.m. on the morning of the sixth and began to issue orders. General Asboth and his division would leave immediately with the wagon train for Little Sugar Creek, and Colonel Osterhaus would then follow with his division.

In spite of the darkness and the cold, the withdrawal went reasonably well, with General Asboth and the trains followed by Colonel Osterhaus's division getting clear of Bentonville by midmorning. Sigel had kept about 600 men and a battery of artillery with him in the town and intended to add Colonel Schaefer's men from Osage Mills to this group, giving him a rear guard of about 1,200 men. Having given orders to that effect, Sigel walked over to the Eagle Hotel on the town square and ordered breakfast. It was about 9:30 a.m. A few minutes later, Colonel Schaefer with his Second Missouri Infantry came into town. Nobody gave Schaefer the order to stay with the rear guard, so he marched his men on out of town toward Little Sugar Creek and Sigel lost half of his planned force.

While his army made themselves as comfortable as possible on the frigid night of March 5, Earl Van Dorn worried about Colonel Greer's skirmish north of town. He finally decided that instead of rushing his cavalry north directly to Bentonville in the morning, he would send most of the mounted men northwest to Osage Mills, in case the Yankees were still there, and march up Bentonville Road with the infantry. Accordingly, at first light, General McIntosh rode off with most of the mounted troops toward Osage Mills, which had already been evacuated, and the footsore infantry fell in on the main road. By changing his plans at the last moment, Van Dorn had just missed his last chance to intercept the main body of Sigel's troops. When Sigel gave the withdrawal order, he also sent a cavalry detachment back south down the Elm Springs Road about five miles to watch for the approaching Southerners. Just after 9:00 a.m., they made contact with the head of the Confederate column, and after a short skirmish, they withdrew back up the road toward Bentonville.

Van Dorn knew that the retiring Yankee cavalry had been set there to raise the alarm, so speed was now his only hope. The infantry were much too slow, so he sent what little cavalry he had kept with him galloping north under the command of Colonel Elijah Gates. Just after 10:00 a.m., three things happened: Franz Sigel came out of the Eagle Hotel to find that Schaefer and the Second Missouri had left town, leaving him with only about six hundred men; the cavalry detachment from the Elm Springs Road came pounding into town and reported that the Confederates were right behind them; and James McIntosh (coming from Osage Mills) and Elijah Gates (coming up the Elm

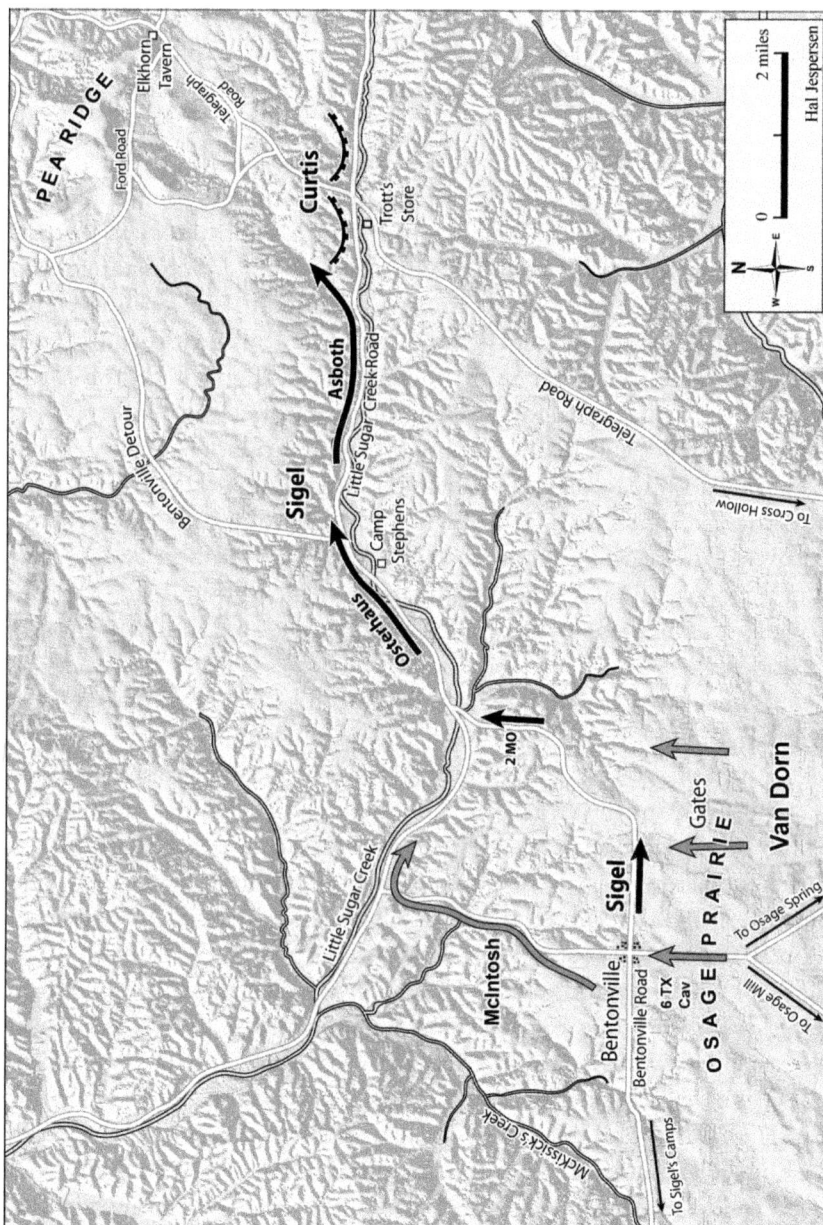

Action around Bentonville on March 6. *Courtesy of Hal Jespersen.*

Springs Road) met and united the Confederate cavalry about two miles south of Bentonville. Brigadier General Franz Sigel, who was in charge of fully half the Federal army, was now caught at the tail end of his own column facing practically the entire Confederate cavalry with a rear guard that amounted to one under-strength regiment. By 10:30 a.m., they were on the move east out of town.

Brigadier General James McIntosh had graduated from West Point (class of 1849) and seemed to favor grand, complicated Napoleonic maneuvers, and that would come back to haunt him on this day. Instead of simply riding east with his entire mounted force to outdistance and then cut off Sigel's slower-moving group, he divided them, sending Gates and his Missouri cavalry to harass Sigel while he took his Texans north through Bentonville to circle behind them and cut them off at the Little Sugar Creek crossing, about four miles northeast of town. Gates did his best, but Sigel's men and artillery kept his Missouri riders at bay, while McIntosh was slowed to a walk in heavier timber near the creek as his men and horses began to break down due to fatigue and the freezing temperatures. One of the Texans wrote, "I was so benumbed by cold that I could not cap my pistols." Sigel kept his men moving and reached the critical creek crossing northeast of Bentonville just ahead of McIntosh's frozen troopers.

After crossing Little Sugar Creek, Sigel and his little band had to stop and unlimber the artillery a few times to keep back McIntosh's attempts to attack or flank him, but each time, Sigel was able to retire successfully. From 10:30 a.m. until about 3:30 p.m., when Colonel Osterhaus countermarched his troops and came to his rescue, Franz Sigel conducted a masterful fighting withdrawal from Bentonville, but it was the job of a regimental commander, not of the head of two full divisions. Why he put himself in that position is still a question today.[68]

While Sigel was evacuating Bentonville, Curtis was also falling back from Cross Hollow. By the time Sigel was eating breakfast, Curtis was back at Little Sugar Creek where Telegraph Road crossed it and had men from Colonel Davis's division hard at work on fortifications atop the bluffs on the north bank. The final unit unaccounted for was Colonel William Vandever's force at Huntsville, and couriers were sent galloping there to recall him. As it happened, Vandever had already heard rumors of the Confederate advance from the local people and had put his men on the road before dawn, only to meet the couriers within a few miles. In what can only be described as a heroic effort, Vandever and his men reached Curtis's position at Little Sugar

Creek that evening, marching forty-two miles in sixteen hours without losing a single man.[69]

By 8:00 p.m. on the sixth, the Federal troops who would fight the battle were in position atop the bluffs that overlooked Telegraph Road as it crossed Little Sugar Creek. The Confederates, after failing to catch Sigel and his rear guard, had moved into an area along Little Sugar Creek they called Camp Stevens, about three miles to the west. As darkness fell, the Confederate army stretched back from Camp Stevens for several miles toward Bentonville, with the food and ammunition wagons far in the rear. They would continue arriving all night. Generals Van Dorn, Price and McCulloch, however, were already planning their next move, which Earl Van Dorn hoped would spell the end of Curtis's army and the beginning of his grand offensive on St. Louis.

Chapter 10

March 7, 1862

Contact

I f ever there was a general who went into a major campaign on the fly, it was Earl Van Dorn. When he arrived in the Boston Mountains and took command of this army on March 3, he had never, as far as we know, met either of his subordinate commanders or set foot in the mountains of northwest Arkansas. He brought only two staff officers with him, neither of which knew any more about the troops or the terrain than he did, and he was sick from the rigors of his travels. Among his advantages were the incredible stamina and courage of the rank and file Confederate soldier and most of his officers, as well as Ben McCulloch's knowledge of the local terrain. McCulloch and his army had marched and camped all over this area the past summer and fall and knew every road, trail and country lane.

Early in the evening of March 6, the Confederate commanders met near Camp Stevens, and Ben McCulloch laid out the situation for Van Dorn. The Federal position at Telegraph Road and Little Sugar Creek was a very strong one. Samuel Curtis, an engineer by trade, had chosen well, and to approach his position head on would be playing into his hand. With the Federals on the bluffs across the creek and artillery firing down, the Little Sugar Creek Valley would be a killing field. Trying to turn their left flank would be little better. Where Curtis was vulnerable was on his right. McCulloch said that there was a "good gravelly road" that led north from Camp Stevens and wandered for about eight miles through the countryside north of the Federal position until it came back to Telegraph Road about three miles north of Elkhorn Tavern. The locals called it the Bentonville Detour.

McCulloch suggested that they might use the Detour to get around Curtis's right, flank him out of his strong position and force him to fall back into Missouri. For maybe the only time in their association, Sterling Price immediately agreed with the Texan. Van Dorn, however, had grander things in mind. Simply forcing the Federals to retreat back into Missouri wouldn't do. By using the Detour, he wanted to get all the way to Telegraph Road in Curtis's rear, cut him off from his supply line and destroy his army. Van Dorn could then march unopposed to Springfield and on to St. Louis, as he had planned. Once he learned about the Detour, the Confederate commander decided to move at once.[70]

When Van Dorn told Price and McCulloch to start the men on the Detour immediately, McCulloch was shocked. He had watched the troops and animals plod in, exhausted after having marched more than fifty miles in freezing weather during the past sixty hours. Most of the men had eaten the last of their rations for breakfast that morning. He strongly urged Van Dorn to let the men have the night to rest and begin in the morning but was unsuccessful.

Samuel Curtis's army was not a band of Comanches whose only thought was escape, as Van Dorn had fought in Texas and Indian Territory before the war, but the same fear now seemed to animate him, as it would another cavalryman named Custer fourteen years later in Montana. Major "Sul" Ross of the Sixth Texas Cavalry, who had known and served under Van Dorn in Texas, recognized the flaw in his thinking. In a letter written after the battle, Ross said, "The truth of the whole matter was, General Van Dorn did not believe the Federals would fight him, but, rather, that they would get away from him."[71]

By 8:00 p.m., the Confederates were on the move again. Many fires were built to give the appearance of a large camp, but in fact, most of the men were falling in on the road. Unfortunately, what Van Dorn hoped would be a smooth and fairly rapid operation soon degenerated into a slogging mess. General McIntosh's cavalry was supposed to lead the way, but Price's men were in front, blocking the road, and from the beginning, the march fell further and further behind schedule. Some of the men had camped on the far side of Little Sugar Creek, and more time was lost as they constructed crude bridges to get across. Van Dorn had hoped to be on Telegraph Road in the rear of the Federal army by sunrise, but that was not to be.

Some of Price's Missouri cavalry force was out front, but the pace of the march was set by Price's trudging infantry, while McIntosh and his horsemen sat on their mounts for six hours in the cold and dark, waiting their turn.

Then came the rest of Ben McCulloch's men, and bringing up the rear were Albert Pike and his Creek and Cherokee Mounted Rifles, who had just arrived. When the sun rose on March 7, the head of the Confederate column had not yet reached Telegraph Road, while the tail had not yet left camp Stevens.

While all of this was going on, the Federals were not idle. Curtis was well aware that the danger was on his right and had refused that end of his line so that it faced to the northwest, just in case. He also knew about the Bentonville Detour, and it worried him, which made Colonel Grenville Dodge's suggestion very welcome. Early in the evening, Colonel Dodge had come to headquarters and suggested that perhaps something should be done to obstruct the Detour, just in case. As with most things in the army, to suggest something is to volunteer for it, and Curtis was happy for Dodge to take part of his Fourth Iowa and go to work. During the evening and early morning, Dodge and his men traveled around the Detour in the opposite direction from the Confederates and cut down trees for two road blocks—one about a mile east of a little country meetinghouse called Twelve Corner Church and one near the junction of the Detour and Telegraph Road. They were gone before any of the Confederates arrived, but the obstacles delayed the Rebels, who were already behind schedule, for several more hours plus let them know that the Federals were aware of their route.[72]

The night march around the Federal position was simply brutal for the Confederate army. All along the Detour, men were falling out of ranks—sometimes whole companies—and lying exhausted and asleep by the side of the road in the freezing temperatures. The bill for the forced marches and short rations of the past few days was coming due. It is one of the enduring ironies of the Pea Ridge Campaign that General Earl Van Dorn, by insisting on the killing pace of the advance to the battlefield, almost certainly created as many casualties among his own men as the Federal army would inflict in almost two days of battle.

First contact was probably made at about 3:00 a.m. when a few Missouri cavalrymen, ranging far out in front of Price's division, approached Telegraph Road on the Detour and captured a Federal picket who later escaped and made his way back to report.[73] It was after sunup when the first Southern riders reached Telegraph Road, and it took Van Dorn another hour to reach them. Having ridden in his ambulance during the night, Van Dorn now mounted his horse to lead his men. By all indications, they had achieved surprise, but something else was also evident: as slow as their progress had been, if all of the troops stayed on the Detour, it would take most of the day

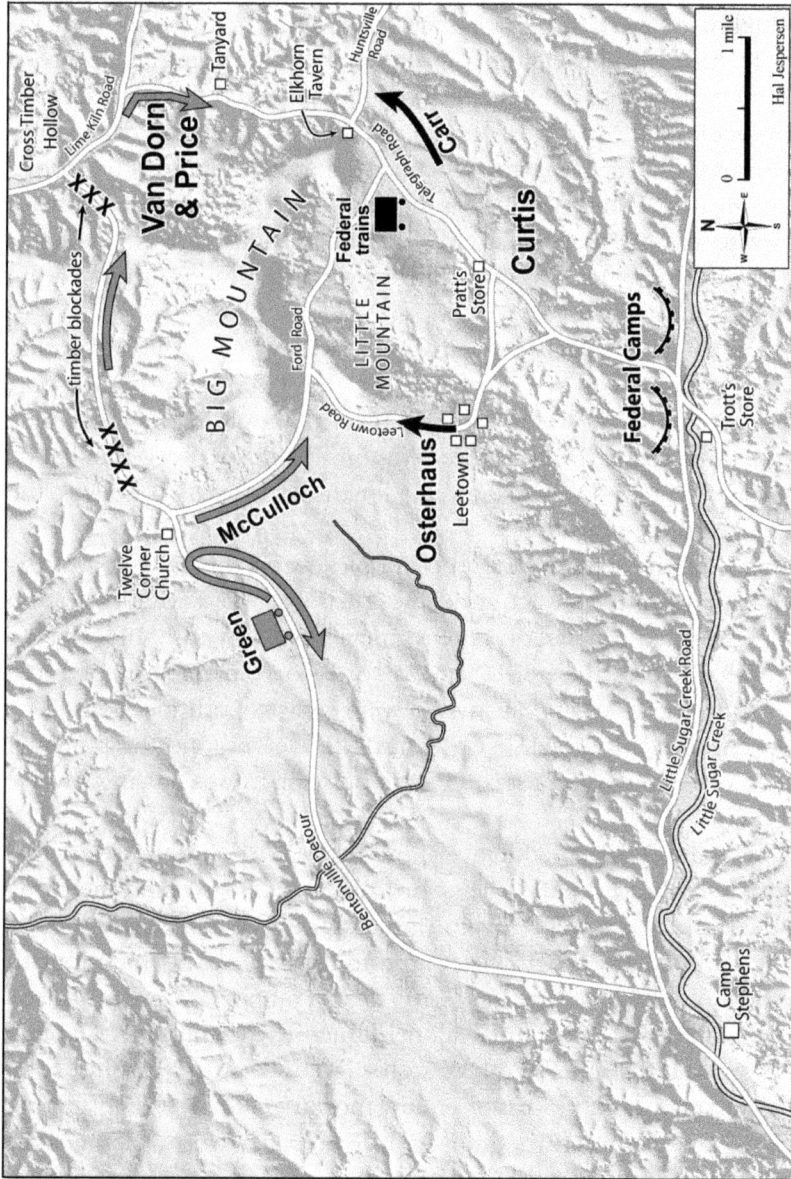

Van Dorn's march around the Federal army (night of March 6–7) and Curtis's initial response (morning of March 7). *Courtesy of Hal Jespersen.*

for them to get there. Sometime during the next few hours, Van Dorn made a decision that may have made sense at the time but would lead to disaster.

Van Dorn decided to divide his army and send General McCulloch's division to Elkhorn Tavern by a more direct route. He sent orders for General McCulloch to turn off the Detour onto a small country lane called Ford Road, after a family whose farm it passed. Not only would this path shorten their march, but unknown to Van Dorn at the time, it would also bring them into the rear area of Curtis's army where, among other things, the supply wagons were located. While waiting for the infantry to get organized, parties of Confederate cavalry began carefully pushing south down Telegraph Road.[74] At about this time, however, things were beginning to move in the Federal camp as well.

When Curtis fell back to Little Sugar Creek the day before, he had posted Major Eli W. Weston with six companies of the Twenty-fourth Missouri and two companies of cavalry at Elkhorn Tavern, about one mile north of his own command post at Pratt's Store. Weston was the provost marshal of Samuel Curtis's army and was responsible for the security of prisoners, the supply wagons and the rear area.

On the night of the sixth, Weston posted pickets on the three roads that intersected at or near the tavern, and by sunrise on the seventh, Weston had already received reports of enemy movement on both the Detour near Telegraph Road to the north and on Ford Road in the area of Little Mountain to the west. Additional troops were sent to both locations. The Confederates on Ford Road fell back toward the Detour, and the pursuing Federals got close enough to observe a large body of troops passing Twelve Corner Church.

The Confederates north of the tavern on Telegraph Road, however, had not yet met any real resistance as Missouri cavalry scouts worked their way slowly south, capturing one of several foraging parties that was out early scouring the countryside. Their luck came to an end about three-fourths of a mile north of Elkhorn Tavern. There, near a tan yard, General Price's escort, commanded by Lieutenant Colonel James T. Cearnal, met Captain Robert W. Fyan and Company B of Weston's Twenty-fourth Missouri. Fyan had been sent to check out reports of enemy movement on Telegraph Road. When Cearnal's horsemen came into sight, Fyan wasn't sure whether they were friend or foe until they fired on a party sent forward to meet them. Private John Franklin was wounded—possibly the first casualty of the battle. Very soon, Fyan and his company were falling back to a better position and calling for reinforcements.[75]

By about 8:00 a.m., Major Weston was standing before General Curtis at his headquarters, reporting in person the actions now going on in the area around the tavern, when Captain Barbour Lewis of the First Missouri Cavalry arrived from the engagement on Ford Road to report his sighting of Confederate troops at Twelve Corner Church. Curtis thanked both officers, sent them back to their commands and immediately sent orders for a meeting of commanders at 9:00 a.m.[76]

The Confederates whom Captain Lewis encountered on Ford Road fell back, but the ones north of the tavern were growing stronger and more aggressive as Van Dorn and Price moved more of their troops off the Detour and down Telegraph Road. In response to Captain Fyan's urgent request, Weston had sent two more companies down to reinforce Company B, and they were holding their own. They soon noticed, however, that Confederate troops were trying to move around their right flank. Fyan took his company through the woods to the Huntsville Road, and Weston moved around the rest of his small infantry and cavalry force, trying to counter the moves, but more Confederates were arriving all the time. If the position around the tavern were to be held, Weston needed help, and very soon.

Major General Earl Van Dorn, commander of the Confederate troops at Pea Ridge.
Modern portrait by John Kiser, courtesy of Ferguson Hall Historic Site, Spring Hill, Tennessee.

While he waited for his commanders to arrive, Samuel Curtis tried to decide what Earl Van Dorn was up to. In spite of the reports of Confederates on Telegraph Road north of the tavern, he was inclined to believe that they were a diversion. To Curtis, the more logical move would be a two-pronged attack— one to turn his right flank by way of the Detour and Ford Road and another to attack his primary position on Little Sugar Creek. Since he was as ready as he could get at the creek, Curtis saw the Confederates around Twelve Corner Church as the primary threat.

Engraving of the Battle of Pea Ridge, published in *Harper's Weekly*. *Author's collection.*

The commanders meeting started with some preliminary discussion as to whether the army should fight or withdraw. Curtis announced that they would stay and fight and then ordered that a division-sized force be sent through the tiny village of Leetown and on toward Twelve Corner Church to observe and, if possible, engage any enemy forces in the area. Command of this force was given to Colonel Peter Osterhaus. The German colonel, along with Colonel Nicholas Greusel, whose brigade would be Osterhaus's infantry, left immediately to carry out the orders.

Believing that he had taken steps to deal with his primary threat, Curtis was surprised to receive an urgent message a few minutes later from Major Weston reporting a heavy column of enemy cavalry, infantry and artillery within a mile of Elkhorn Tavern. Curtis was still not quite prepared to believe that Van Dorn would have sent such a large force on such a long nighttime march, but obviously Weston's provost guard—essentially an under-strength regiment—was not sufficient to deal with the threat in front of them.[77]

The initial contact had been made by Confederate cavalrymen, who had dismounted to spar with Captain Fyan and his reinforced company down in the hollow near the tan yard, but soon after 10:00 a.m., Van Dorn and Price arrived at the head of the infantry and artillery. This was what had prompted Major Weston's second message. At this point, however, the normally very aggressive Earl Van Dorn did something very uncharacteristic. Instead of immediately pressing up the road with Colonel Henry Little's First Missouri Brigade, which was the leading infantry unit, he ordered General Price to stop and deploy his troops in line of battle and move forward cautiously. Van Dorn, who had pressed the army so hard to get to this point, suddenly seemed tentative. He had no way of knowing that the area around Elkhorn Tavern was, at the time, held only by Major Weston's provost guard. By stopping to deploy at this critical time, Van Dorn allowed Curtis time to react before it was too late to save the position at the tavern.[78]

Author's note: From this point, for the rest of March 7, 1862, the Battle of Pea Ridge essentially becomes two separate battles, fought about two miles apart—one around Elkhorn Tavern and the other just north of the small hamlet of Leetown. For several hours in the middle of the day, both fights were going on simultaneously, out of sight but within hearing of each other.

Chapter 11

Elkhorn Tavern

10:30 a.m. to 1:00 p.m.

After receiving Major Weston's message about the Confederates near Elkhorn Tavern, Samuel Curtis stepped out of his tent near Pratt's Store and happened to see a large body of troops drawn up nearby. After his mission the night before to build the roadblocks, Colonel Grenville Dodge became convinced that an attack was coming on the army's rear area. On his own authority, Dodge had pulled his brigade out of the line at Little Sugar Creek that morning and marched the men a mile or so back to Curtis's headquarters, where they now stood. The army commander may well have been going in search of just such troops to send to the tavern when he stepped out into the sunshine. Finding them waiting a few yards away was his good fortune and may have saved Dodge a reprimand for leaving his post. Colonel Eugene A. Carr, Dodge's division commander, was still at Curtis's headquarters, so he was ordered to take Dodge's brigade, hurry to the tavern and take command there.

Major Eli Weston had been juggling his small force and defending the ground around Elkhorn Tavern as best he could for almost three hours while the enemy force grew in front of him. Soon after his troops became engaged, Weston had ordered Captain J.R. Vanzant, with his Company K, to begin moving the prisoners and the provost marshal wagons, which were parked in a field near the tavern, back to a safe area. Now, when Colonel Carr arrived, just before 11:00 a.m. with the Fourth Iowa, the Thirty-fifth Illinois, two battalions of the Third Illinois Cavalry and a six-gun battery of the First Iowa artillery (about 1,250 men), Weston was, in his own words, "somewhat relieved."[79]

Left: Colonel Grenville M. Dodge, commander of the Federal First Brigade, Fourth Division. His brigade held the right flank at Elkhorn Tavern on March 7. *Courtesy of the Library of Congress.*

Below: Telegraph Road as it descends into Cross Timber Hollow just north of Elkhorn Tavern, modern view. Eugene Carr positioned four guns of the First Iowa Battery a few hundred yards down this road on March 7. *Author's collection.*

It didn't take long for Eugene Carr to realize that he had his work cut out for him. As he left for the tavern, General Curtis, still believing that it was a relatively small diversionary force, assured Carr that he could "clean out that hollow in a short time." Seeing the situation for himself, Carr wasn't so sure. Eugene Asa Carr had graduated from West Point in 1850 and had fought Indians before the war. He had developed a reputation as a difficult subordinate but a tough fighter. Due to his intense nature and dark facial hair, his nickname among his fellow officers was "the Black Bearded Cossack." Fortunately for Samuel Curtis, he had sent the right man to Elkhorn Tavern. He would need a "Cossack" there before the day was over.[80]

Since Weston had reported the Confederates moving to his right, Carr's first deployment was to send the cavalry along with Colonel Dodge's Fourth Iowa and two guns of the First Iowa Battery out the Huntsville Road near Clemon's Farm to cover the right flank. Carr left two more guns at the tavern as reserves and then, hoping to buy some time, took the last two guns down the Telegraph Road himself.[81]

Gathering at Elkhorn Tavern, circa 1880. *Courtesy of Pea Ridge National Military Park.*

As it passes Elkhorn Tavern, Telegraph Road starts a descent several hundred feet into a gorge that forms the Arkansas end of Cross Timbers Hollow. The sides of the gorge were fairly steep and covered with brush and timber, but about halfway to the bottom—about four hundred yards from the tavern—Carr found a clear area where he set up his guns to command the road. By now, the Confederates were moving on both sides of the road with infantry. Colonel Henry Little's First Missouri Brigade was astride Telegraph Road, and Colonel William Y. Slack's Second Brigade was moving slowly up the slopes to Little's right. To Little's left were Missouri State Guard units. Carr's Iowa gunners opened fire and stopped the infantry's advance but also prompted Van Dorn to call forward some artillery of his own. Captain Henry Guibor's battery being close at hand, it was soon wrestled up the slopes to a good position and began to duel with the Yankee artillerymen.

Colonel William Y. Slack, commander of the Confederate Second Missouri Brigade. Mortally wounded west of Elkhorn Tavern. *www.generalsandbrevets.com.*

Once Carr began to receive the counter battery fire from the Confederate guns, he immediately sent for the other two guns at the tavern and for Colonel Gustavus A. Smith and his small Thirty-fifth Illinois to support the battery. He also sent a messenger to Curtis, requesting that the rest of his Fourth Division—Colonel William Vandever's brigade—be sent forward immediately. In the meantime, Major Weston recovered the scattered companies of his Twenty-fourth Missouri provost guard and took a position west of the tavern.

Now with four guns, Carr was able to keep the road clear for a while, but the enemy to his left and right were making him and his men pay. Shortly after noon, Dodge's men along Huntsville Road threw back the Confederates' first attempt to turn their right flank, but Carr's position down in the gorge was becoming untenable. In the middle of all this, General Curtis paid his first visit to the tavern. He conferred quickly with Colonel Carr and headed back to gather more reinforcements.

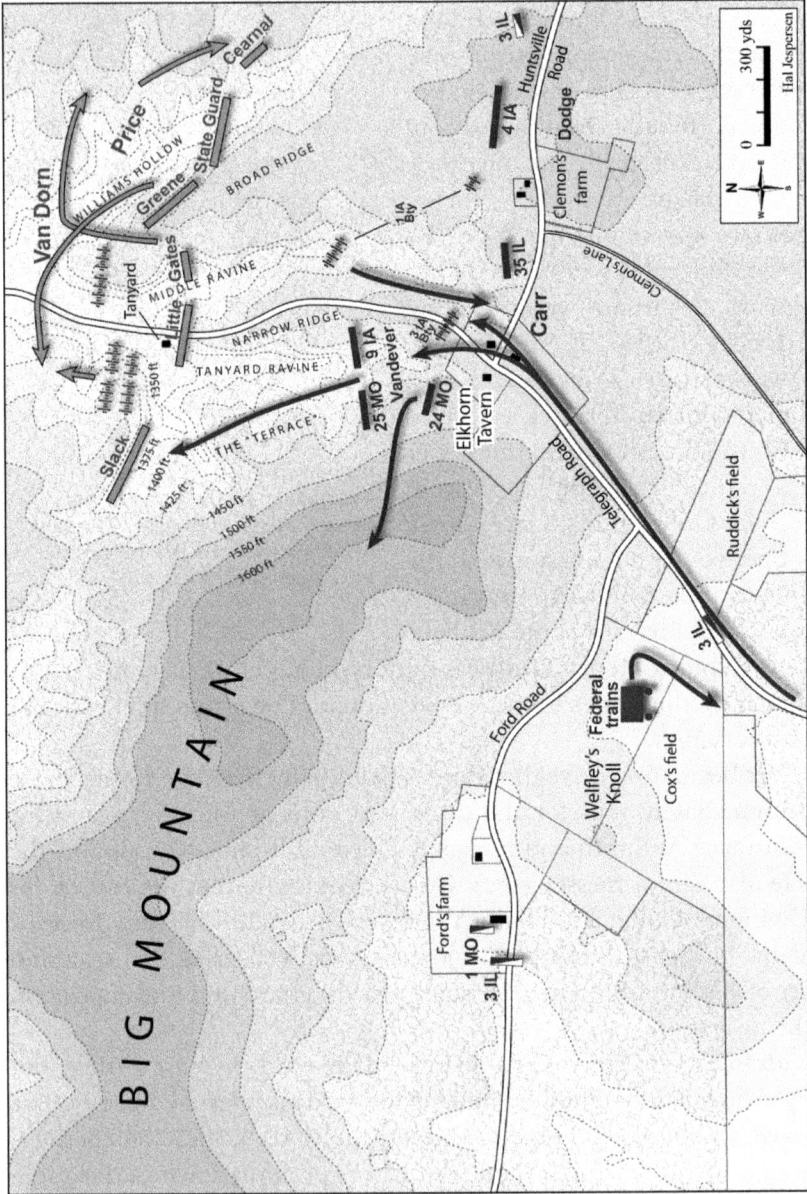

Elkhorn Tavern midday on March 7. Carr goes into position facing Van Dorn and Price. Vandever arrives to reinforce Carr. *Courtesy of Hal Jespersen.*

Colonel Eugene Asa Carr, commander of the Federal Fourth Division. Carr, with his division, held Elkhorn Tavern for almost seven hours on March 7. *Courtesy of the Library of Congress.*

By about 12:30 p.m., all but one of Carr's guns had been disabled, several ammunition chests had been destroyed and several men and horses had been killed or wounded, so he finally withdrew back to the tavern, where a battery of the Third Iowa Artillery had now arrived in advance of Vandever's brigade and gone to action. Colonel Smith of the Thirty-fifth Illinois had been hit twice and had his horse killed under him. Colonel Carr himself had been wounded three times but remained on the field. He and his little band of Iowa gunners were badly beaten up, but the Confederates had not advanced up the road.

Soon, the rest of Colonel William Vandever's Second Brigade began arriving—the Ninth Iowa and the Twenty-fifth Missouri. Vandever was sent to the west of the tavern to join Weston's tiny force that was facing a large body of Confederates moving through the brush to the west of Telegraph Road near the base of a large ridge called Big Mountain. This was Colonel Slack's Second Brigade, still trying to climb out of Tanyard Ravine.[82] For a little while, however, there was a lull in the fighting.

By noon, Van Dorn had most of Sterling Price's Missouri troops on the field but was running into problems of his own. Moving large formations of troops and pulling artillery through the brush that covered the hillsides and ravines was difficult and time-consuming, and coordinating their movements over such a large area was next to impossible. Van Dorn was also expecting to hear the firing of McCulloch's division soon as it arrived in the enemy's rear.

For the time being, Earl Van Dorn was content to position his forces for the all-out assault that would crush the Federals opposing him around Elkhorn Tavern between the two halves of his army. Two miles to the west, however, Colonel Peter Osterhaus was about to upset those plans.

Chapter 12

Leetown

11:30 a.m. to 1:30 p.m.

THE FEDERALS

By 11:30 a.m., Colonel Peter J. Osterhaus's operation against what General
Curtis considered the primary threat was well underway. The advance units of
the force he had put together consisted of about six hundred cavalry—battalions
of Third Iowa and the First and Fifth Missouri Cavalry. Along with them came
three guns of the First Missouri Flying Battery under Captain G.M. Elbert. This
force was followed by Colonel Nicholas Greusel and his infantry brigade—the
Thirty-sixth Illinois, Twelfth Missouri and Twenty-second Indiana, plus two
more artillery batteries. As Osterhaus caught up with the head of his column,
the men were north of Leetown passing a large open field on the west side of
Leetown Road that was known as Oberson's Field after one of the local men
who farmed it.

Colonel Osterhaus still knew nothing about the enemy force supposed
to be in front of him and so decided to go on ahead with the cavalry force
to scout toward Twelve Corner Church. Upon seeing Oberson's Field,
however, he decided that the infantry should deploy along its south side and
form a solid fallback position until more was known about the force they
might be facing. It was the best defensive position around, offering good
fields of fire for several hundred yards to the north and west, as well as
commanding the Leetown Road. Leaving a staff officer to direct Colonel
Greusel into position, Osterhaus led the cavalry forward. Off to the east, the

Federal position along the south edge of Oberson's Field, March 7, modern view. *Author's collection.*

sound of artillery could be heard as Colonel Carr arrived at Elkhorn Tavern and went into action.

A band of trees and brush along the north side of Oberson's Field blocked the view toward Twelve Corner Church, but a little farther up the Leetown Road, Osterhaus found a country lane running west through the timber. It was called Foster's Lane, and the cavalry turned into it, hoping that it would lead through the woods to more open country beyond. About half a mile later, Foster's Lane turned north and came out of the trees and into open fields. It was here, sometime just before noon, where Peter Osterhaus's most important question was answered.

As Colonel Osterhaus and his small cavalry force rode out of the trees, the sight in front of them almost took their breath away. A few hundred yards to the north ran Ford Road, and it was completely filled with Ben McCulloch's entire division. Louis Hebert's infantry brigade was in the lead, nearing the low pass between Big Mountain and Little Mountain, and McIntosh's mounted troops were riding through the north edge of the fields beside them. Colonel Osterhaus realized immediately that the head of McCulloch's column was only a mile or so from the fields where the army's supply train was parked, as well as Curtis's headquarters.

As he later noted in his official report: "Notwithstanding my command was entirely inadequate to the overwhelming masses opposed to me...I could not hesitate in my course of action. The safety of our position was dependent upon the securing of our right flank and the keeping back of the enemy until I was re-enforced."[83]

Osterhaus ordered the three James Rifles of Elbert's battery to open fire as soon as possible. The Confederate column had to be stopped or turned, whatever the cost.

THE CONFEDERATES

General Ben McCulloch received General Van Dorn's order to turn off the Detour sometime after 10:00 a.m. Ford Road turned right off the Detour a hundred yards or so past Twelve Corner Church, and when Van Dorn's courier found General McCulloch, a good portion of his division was already past the turnoff. Valuable time was lost countermarching his troops and getting them turned onto Ford Road, with Pike and his Indians tacked on to the rear.

As they finally began to get organized, artillery fire began to be heard to the east. Colonel Carr had "opened the ball" against Van Dorn and Price near Elkhorn Tavern. This caused McCulloch to halt his troops yet again and redeploy them into a formation that could go more quickly from the march to a battle line. His infantry and artillery would march on Ford Road, with Louis Hebert's brigade leading the way, while his mounted troops, under McIntosh, would travel in the fields to their right with Pike and the Indians bringing up the rear. While this made good sense tactically, the delay proved to be a fatal error, both for McCulloch and his division. Finally on the move again, these troops composed well over half of Van Dorn's army. Even with the attrition caused by the forced march and freezing weather, McCulloch's division still numbered almost seven thousand men.[84]

It was now nearing noon, and the head of McCulloch's column was approaching a saddle between Big Mountain on its left and Little Mountain on its right, with McIntosh's cavalry trotting along beside the men through the edge of a large field belonging to a man named Foster. In less than two miles, McCulloch's men would be in the left rear of Eugene Carr's hard-pressed division around Elkhorn Tavern that was contesting Price and Van Dorn's advance up Telegraph Road, as well as among the Federal trains that were in the fields just over the hill—just as Earl Van Dorn had planned.

Foster's Farm from Elbert's Federal battery, modern view. The Confederates were positioned along Ford Road in the distance, and Little Mountain is just out of view to the right. *Author's collection.*

The first volley from the First Missouri's three James Rifles came as a complete surprise to the Confederate column. No one had noticed the small Federal battery with its cavalry supports as it set up and opened fire, and for a few moments all was confusion. Soon, however, the units were reacting. Louis Hebert's men put their heads down below the fence rails as the grapeshot rattled around them and moved quickly on down the road to the woods. James McIntosh simply wheeled his cavalry around to face the threat.[85]

Captain John J. Good and his Texas battery were on the road when the first shells burst about fifty yards away. He managed to get one of his pieces in action and returned one shot—the only Confederate battery to reply to the initial Federal barrage.[86] General McCulloch quickly made his way to General McIntosh and ordered a charge on the enemy battery, which McIntosh was already organizing. Colonel Osterhaus had gotten the Confederates' attention, but now he faced a force that outnumbered his little band by about six to one—and those were just the mounted troops.

While the Confederate cavalrymen were turning to their right to face the battery, the Federal guns kept up their fire. Soon, however, the sound

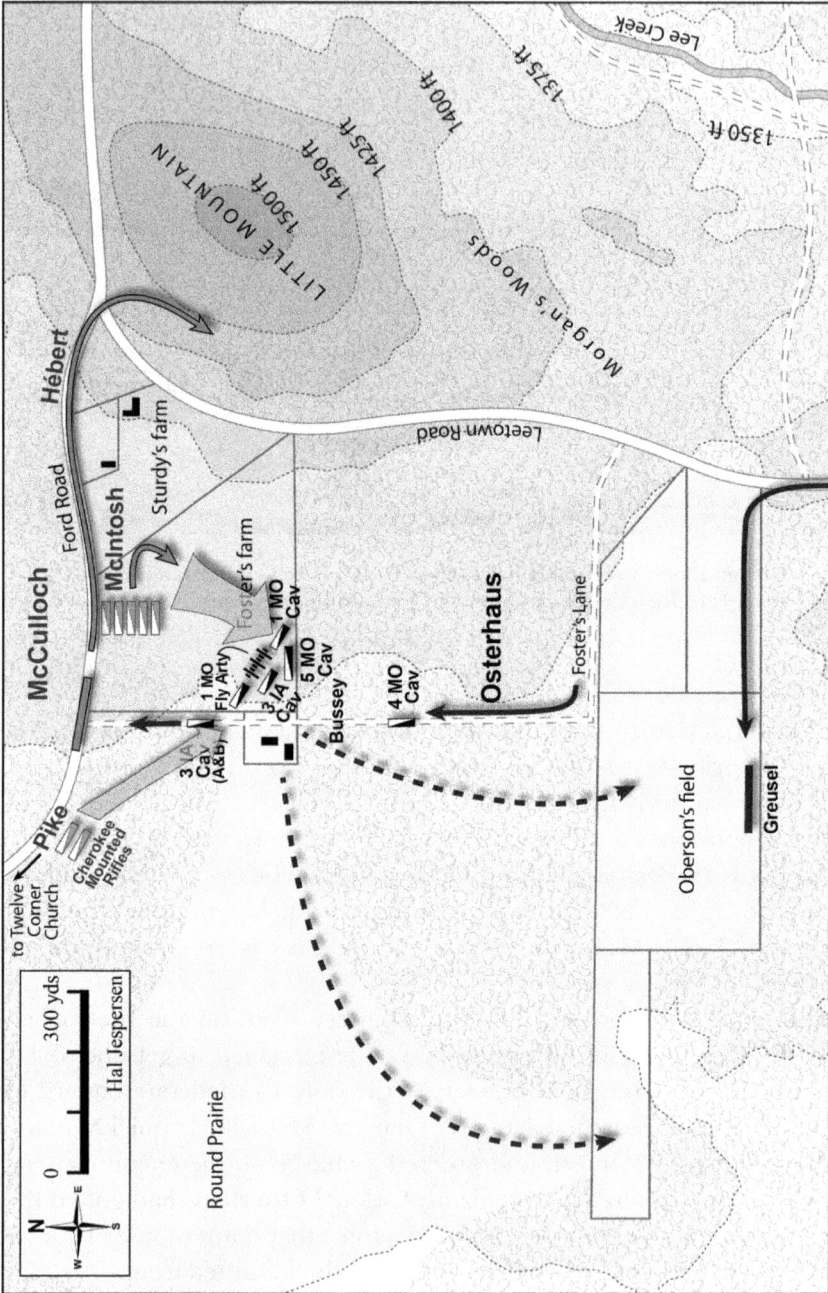

Leetown, noon on March 7. Osterhaus fires on McCulloch's division at Foster's Farm. *Courtesy of Hal Jespersen.*

of bugles could be heard, and something over three thousand Texas and Arkansas riders surged across the open field toward the Federal guns in a classic Napoleon-style cavalry charge. Elbert's men got off eighteen rounds before the mass of Confederate horsemen enveloped them. Henry Dysart of the Third Iowa Cavalry, which tried to support the battery, survived the encounter and later tried to make some sense of it in his diary:

> *I have read in history of, and seen depicted the horrors of battle, where foe measured arms with foe in mortal combat, but here my own eyes witnessed them. In every direction I could see my comrades falling...Men and horses ran in collision, crushing each other to the ground...Officers tried to rally their men, but order gave way to confusion. The scene baffles description.*[87]

Just before the Confederate charge came, Colonel Osterhaus had sent Companies A and B of the Third Iowa under Lieutenant Colonel Trimble up Foster Lane to attack what probably looked like the rear of the Confederate column. They were about three hundred yards to the northwest and escaped the main assault only to run head on into Albert Pike's Creek and Cherokee troops, who were trailing the column. In what was surely one of the most bizarre scenes in the Civil War, almost one thousand mounted and dismounted Indians came screaming out of the woods and swept over the two small companies of Iowa cavalry. Colonel Trimble was wounded and many other saddles emptied, and soon the rest of the Yankee troopers were in flight back up Foster Lane—all except one. In the middle of the melee, Private Albert Powers wheeled his mount, rode back into the fight, picked up a dismounted trooper and carried him safely back. For this, Powers would be awarded the Medal of Honor.[88] During the fight, a few of the Indians fell back into some of their old habits. After the battle, Federal soldiers would discover that several of the Third Iowa casualties had been scalped and mutilated.[89]

Colonel Osterhaus told Colonel Cyrus Bussey to save what he could of the cavalry and then fell back down Foster Lane through the trees to Oberson's Field, followed closely by a stampede from the battle behind him. Colonel Nicholas Greusel's infantry was just filing into place on the south edge of Oberson's Field when a large group of wild-eyed cavalrymen and riderless horses, some with bloody and empty saddles, came through the lines, causing quite an uproar and almost trampling some of the foot soldiers. Osterhaus was afraid that the retreat of the cavalry might panic the infantry, but Colonel Greusel held them steady, and once the stampede had passed, they took their positions.

Once the charge was over in Foster's Field, most of McIntosh's Confederates and Pike's Indians milled around the captured cannons. One of the few who pursued the fleeing Yankee troopers was Major "Sul" Ross and some of his men from the Sixth Texas. As he rode southwest after the fleeing Federals, Ross came to the south edge of the band of timber and saw what looked to him like several thousand infantry and artillery in Oberson's Field. They saw Ross and his small group of Texans, too, and one of Greusel's batteries unlimbered and lofted a few shells their way. Ross and the Texans fell back into the trees, and he later said, "I did not run, but I walked very fast!" Within a few minutes, he would be reporting what he had seen to Ben McCulloch.[90]

Chapter 13

"My God, It's Poor Old Ben!"

Ross's report forced a difficult decision on Ben McCulloch. Far from being just a scouting party, this small band of cavalry with the single battery that had stopped the Confederate column now appeared to be just the advance unit of a much larger enemy force. Obviously he couldn't continue to march toward Elkhorn Tavern with such a force in his rear, so Ben McCulloch decided to start his part of the battle right where he was. Accordingly, he called for a quick meeting with his two senior subordinates, James McIntosh and Louis Hebert, and ordered the infantry to leave the road and form up in the field facing south.

While McCulloch was organizing his troops and meeting with his commanders, Peter Osterhaus considered his situation. Although they had not shown themselves yet, he felt sure that he had succeeded in bringing the Confederates' attention onto himself and his small force. The problem now would be to hold until help could arrive. Osterhaus had already sent a rider in search of General Curtis, reporting his encounter with McCulloch's division and requesting reinforcements as soon as possible. At the moment, he had three regiments and nine pieces of artillery in Oberson's Field—about 1,600 men plus whatever of the shattered cavalry units might manage to reform. Against him, McCulloch could bring about 4,000 infantry plus McIntosh's 3,000 mounted troops and four batteries of artillery.

As the Confederate units marched off Ford Road and formed up at the edge of the timber facing south, they were separated from the Federals by about eight hundred yards—about four hundred yards of timber and brush immediately in front of them and then four hundred yards of open ground across Oberson's Field. Just to keep the pressure on, some of the Federal guns began to lob shots blindly over the belt of trees to fall among the Confederate units. Even though they were not aimed, the Federal shells began to cause casualties among the Rebel troops. Captain John Good's Texas battery, near Ford Road, replied in kind, and the Federal and Confederate artillery continued their indirect duel off and on for several hours.

At the brief meeting of the three senior Confederate commanders, McCulloch explained his plan. In Foster's Field and the prairie to the west, he had placed, from west to east, the Sixteenth and Seventeenth Arkansas regiments, the Second and then the First Arkansas Mounted Rifles (dismounted) and, finally, the Fourth Texas Cavalry nearest the Leetown Road. This force would be commanded by McCulloch personally. East of the Leetown Road, in an area known locally as Morgan's Woods, Colonel Louis Hebert had four infantry regiments: Colonel Evander McNair's Fourth Arkansas nearest the road; Hebert's own Third Louisiana, now led by Major W.H. Tunnard; Colonel William C. Mitchell's Fourteenth Arkansas; and Colonel Dandridge McRae's Fifteenth Arkansas. These troops east of the road would be commanded by Hebert and, since they couldn't see the action to the west, were to advance once they heard the battle commence on that side of the road. In Foster's Field behind the front line, General McIntosh had four cavalry regiments in a second line: the First Arkansas, and the First, Ninth and Eleventh Texas. The Sixth Texas covered Good's battery, and the Third Texas took a position on the upper slopes of Little Mountain. Pike's Creek and Cherokee troops formed in the rear of McIntosh, and the remaining three batteries stayed on Ford Road.[91]

It had taken the Confederates some time to get organized for their attack. In the meantime, the Federals were making their dispositions. Colonel Greusel soon decided to put some eyes on the far side of the large field in front of his Thirty-sixth Illinois. With more than eight hundred men, it was by far the largest regiment on the field. In fact, sometime during the lull while the Confederates were forming up beyond the trees, several groups of Federals ventured across Oberson's Field to the edge of the timber. One group from the Twelfth Missouri succeeded in recovering a howitzer that had been left behind in the cavalry's retreat, and the Thirty-sixth Illinois deployed two companies across to the fence line on the north edge of the field to act as skirmishers.[92]

Captain Silas Miller and his men of Company B, Thirty-sixth Illinois, crossed Oberson's Field and deployed along the fence line on the north side. They were followed by Captain Irving W. Parkhurst's Company G, which was to cover them. As the two companies went into position along the fence line, just beyond the line of timber in front of them, Ben McCulloch was about to launch his attack. It was about 1:30 p.m.[93]

As Ben McCulloch prepared to begin, he rode to the right of his line to the position of the Sixteenth Arkansas. He told Colonel John Hill to start two companies forward as skirmishers and to follow with the full regiment if any resistance was encountered. The general then said that he was going farther to the right to try to get a closer look at the Federal line for himself. Ben McCulloch had been a soldier and Indian fighter for twenty-five years. He had fought with Sam Houston at San Jacinto, scouted for the army during the Mexican-American War and fought Indians as a Texas Ranger. Doing his own reconnaissance was an old habit that hadn't changed since he had become a general. He had done what he was about to do a hundred times before.

As McCulloch and a few of his staff passed to the right of the Sixteenth Arkansas skirmishers and approached a sort of clearing in the underbrush, he told the rest to stay back. "Your grey horses will attract the fire of the sharpshooters," he said. On his sorrel, he rode forward alone until he had a vantage point on a small rise and took out his spyglass. Unknown to the general or anyone else on his side of the field, he was now only seventy yards or so from the Thirty-sixth Illinois skirmishers who had occupied the fence line a few minutes earlier. Sitting on his horse, dressed in his black velvet suit (McCulloch never wore a uniform) and outlined against the sky, he made a perfect target. Captain Miller had no idea who the lone rider was, but he never hesitated. He gave the order, his men fired a volley and Brigadier General Benjamin McCulloch was dead before he hit the ground, shot through the heart.[94]

The volley that killed McCulloch also took the Arkansas skirmishers by surprise, but they didn't see the general fall. The Illinois men went over the fence and drove the Confederates back into the timber, while a small group went to check on the officer they had seen fall. Part of the group was Private Peter Pelican, who would later claim to be the one who fired the fatal shot. They found McCulloch lying on his back and immediately took his gold watch, his telescope and his Morse rifle, and they were working on his boots when, following McCulloch's last orders, Colonel Hill appeared with the entire Sixteenth Arkansas.[95]

Now it was the Illinois boys' turn to run. As they hurried back to the fence, a brisk firefight began at the edge of the belt of trees, with the Federal artillery soon joining in. Colonel Hill couldn't understand why he had gotten no more orders until, a few minutes into the skirmish, some of his men finally found the general's body. While a messenger went to tell General McIntosh that he was now in command, Colonel Hill advanced his regiment and put more pressure on the two companies of Federal skirmishers.

With the entire Sixteenth Arkansas coming toward him, Captain Miller decided to make a run for it back across Oberson's Field while he had the chance. Before he and his men were halfway across, however, the Arkansas men ran to the fence line and delivered a volley that caused Miller and his men to go to the ground. Now they were pinned down in the open between the two lines. Seeing this, Colonel Greusel decided to simply

Brigadier General Benjamin McCulloch, commander of the Confederate division at Leetown. Killed by Federal skirmishers from the Thirty-sixth Illinois on March 7. *Author's collection.*

advance the rest of the Thirty-sixth Illinois and go get them. When the main body of the regiment arrived in the middle of the field a few minutes later, Captain Miller and his men gathered their wounded and hurried to the rear while more than seven hundred Yankee muskets hammered the fence line. Colonel Hill and his men began to take punishment from the fire of the Thirty-sixth but soon noticed movement in the brush to their left. Another Confederate unit was coming forward to help.

When the messenger made it back to Foster's Field with the news of General McCulloch's death, James McIntosh took command of the division, but he didn't immediately order the attack that had been planned. Instead, he told the commanders of the mounted troops in the second line to stand by for orders and then rode forward alone to the Second Arkansas Mounted Rifles, his old regiment. Both the First and Second Arkansas had been dismounted and were now acting as infantry. McIntosh stopped to confer with their commander, Colonel Benjamin T. Embry, and then sent couriers off to order the rest of the frontline units forward. Without waiting for the rest, however, he moved the

Second Arkansas forward himself. These were the troops the men of the Sixteenth Arkansas saw coming up on their left.

The men of the Second Arkansas, normally mounted troops, were worn out from almost four days of marching. "Our regiment was nearly all broke down when we went into the fight," said one of the Arkansas men, "but we done the best we could."[96] When the Second Arkansas emerged from the trees, some of the Federal artillery shifted their fire toward them. General McIntosh, who had been riding in the rear with Colonel Embry, now decided to come around to the right flank. Colonel Greusel also saw the new troops appear and immediately ordered several companies on the right of the Thirty-sixth Illinois to shift their fire toward the new threat. Their volley came just as McIntosh rode into the clear, and the Confederates lost their second commander within minutes of the first.

None of the Confederates saw Ben McCulloch fall, but James McIntosh died in full view of an entire regiment. Colonel Embry, shaken by McIntosh's death, decided to withdraw his exhausted men in the face of the Federal artillery and small-arms fire. This left the Sixteenth Arkansas unsupported, and they soon fell back also. On the way back to Foster's Field, Hill and Embry met the other three units beginning their advance, and after a quick conference, the five regimental commanders decided that they would all fall back and wait for new orders.

Brigadier General James M. McIntosh, commander of the mounted troops in McCulloch's division. Killed at Leetown on March 7. *www.generalsandbrevets.com.*

Command of the division now passed to Colonel Louis Hebert, the senior surviving officer, but he was out of contact. Hearing the firing to his west, he assumed that the general attack had commenced and was advancing his four regiments through Morgan's Woods, following the last orders he had received from McCulloch. He would fight the rest of the day without ever finding out that the two generals were dead and that command of the division had passed to him. Meanwhile, all the Confederates west of Leetown Road had fallen back into Foster's Field, waiting for orders that would never come.

Chapter 14

Morgan's Woods

T he withdrawal of the two Arkansas regiments back into the timber brought on a nervous lull in Oberson's Field. The enemy had fallen back along the line in the Federal front, but unknown to them yet, Hebert's brigade was advancing toward their unsupported right flank east of the Leetown Road. Also unknown to Colonel Peter Osterhaus, a little drama had already played out at General Curtis's headquarters that would prove to be critical to him and his men.

Sometime after 12:30 p.m., Samuel Curtis returned to his headquarters near Pratt's Store after visiting Colonel Carr at Elkhorn Tavern. Curtis was still puzzled as to Van Dorn's plan, but he had seen enough at the tavern to know that Carr needed help. Accordingly, he sent a courier to Little Sugar Creek to find Colonel Jefferson C. Davis and deliver orders for him to take most of his Third Division to Elkhorn Tavern. Soon after the rider left, however, the courier from Colonel Osterhaus arrived, reporting the encounter with McCulloch's entire division north of Leetown and urgently requesting help. Curtis now had to make a decision and make it quickly: support Carr or support Osterhaus? From the beginning, Curtis had considered the threat to his west, from the Detour at Twelve Corner Church, as the most serious, so he sent a second rider after the courier to Davis with a change of orders, directing him to go instead to Leetown and reinforce Osterhaus. Carr and his men would have to hold on a little longer.[97]

In Morgan's Woods, Louis Hebert soon found out how difficult it was to keep four regiments on line while advancing through a dense scrub oak

The Civil War Fight for the Ozarks

Leetown, 1:00 p.m. to 3:00 p.m. on March 7. McCulloch and McIntosh killed. Confederates advance through Morgan's Woods. Davis arrives to reinforce Osterhaus. *Courtesy of Hal Jespersen.*

93

thicket. After a couple of halts to realign as best they could, they were finally approaching Osterhaus's unsupported right flank when part of the Fourth Arkansas, nearest the Leetown Road, was forced out of the woods and into the open. They quickly caught the attention of the Federal batteries in Oberson's Field, which launched a volley of solid shot and canister. This caused Colonel McNair to order his men to fall back into the woods by the left flank. In doing so, they regained the shelter of the timber but also scrambled the regiment with the Third Louisiana as companies intermingled, causing more delay.

Just about this time (2:00 p.m.), Colonel Davis arrived at the head of his division, to Colonel Osterhaus's great relief. Even though Davis was now the senior Federal officer on the field, he agreed that he and Osterhaus should remain in command of their own troops. At Osterhaus's request, Davis then moved his Second Brigade (the Thirty-seventh and Fifty-ninth Illinois—together about nine hundred men), under Colonel Junius White, into the woods east of the Leetown Road to face Louis Hebert's force of about two thousand. Once the Second Brigade was engaged in the underbrush, Davis would send part of his First Brigade (the Eighteenth and Twenty-second Indiana), under Colonel Thomas Pattison, along a woodland path to the east, with orders to pass behind the Second Brigade and attack the Confederates' left flank.[98]

The visibility in the dense thickets east of the road was generally less than fifty yards, so cooperation between units on either side was very difficult. Not long after entering the woods, the Thirty-seventh and Fifty-ninth Illinois lost contact, and each would fight on its own. A few minutes later, the Third Louisiana and the Fourth Arkansas collided with the Thirty-seventh Illinois. To the east in the dense

Colonel Peter J. Osterhaus, commander of the Federal First Division under Franz Sigel. Attacked McCulloch's division north of Leetown on March 7. *Courtesy of the Library of Congress.*

brush, the Fourteenth and Fifteenth Arkansas found the Fifty-ninth Illinois, and the Battle of Morgan's Woods was on. William Watson of the Third Louisiana remembered: "Suddenly, something like a tremendous peal of thunder opened all along our front, and a ridge of fire and smoke appeared close before us, and the trees round us and over our heads rattled with bullets as if in a heavy hail storm."[99]

The first volleys of the Federals staggered the Rebel line, but the men soon recovered, and under officers like Louis Hebert and Evander McNair, they began to push forward. The Confederates much preferred fighting at close quarters, where their shorter-range muskets and shotguns became very lethal, so the underbrush and timber suited them. The underbrush also held another advantage for the Rebels. Again, William Watson: "Our advancing upon them kept us enveloped in the dense smoke while their falling back kept them in the clear atmosphere…Our men squatted down when loading…and looking along under the smoke could take good aim, while the enemy, firing at random into the smoke, much of their shot passed over our heads."[100]

Colonel Louis Hebert, commander of the Confederate infantry brigade in Ben McCulloch's division. Hebert led the Confederate attack through Morgan's Woods at Leetown on March 7. *www.generalsandbrevets.com.*

Under these conditions, the four Confederate and two Federal regiments flailed away at one another for almost an hour, with the superior weight of Confederate numbers slowly forcing both Federal regiments to give ground. The Thirty-seventh fell back toward the southeast corner of Oberson's Field at Leetown Road, while the Fifty-ninth fell back into the dense woods to the south. All during the fight, both the Federal batteries and Captain John Good's Confederate guns lobbed shells blindly into the woods, wounding friend and foe alike.

Finally, as it approached 3:00 p.m., Colonel Davis ordered his two battered regiments to withdraw back into the southeast corner of Oberson's Field. This the Thirty-seventh Illinois managed to do, in a disorganized fashion, but the Fifty-ninth simply fell back farther to the south, deeper into the woods, actually passing some of the Twenty-second Indiana as it filed down the path toward the left flank of the enemy. The Fourteenth and Fifteenth

Arkansas remained in the woods as the Fifty-ninth withdrew from their front, but most of the Third Louisiana and the Fourth Arkansas followed the Thirty-seventh Illinois toward the road.

As the survivors of the Thirty-seventh Illinois came out of the woods, a few companies fell in to support Captain Peter Davidson's six guns of Battery A, Second Illinois Light Artillery (Peoria Battery), which were set up along the road facing the woods. Once the Illinois boys had cleared their line of fire, the battery began blasting the Louisiana and Arkansas men now arriving at the tree line. Although they had been firing all along, the Confederates could now see the guns, and several hundred of them, very loosely led by Colonel McNair, poured out of the woods and charged toward the battery.

For a few minutes, pandemonium reigned along the Leetown Road in the center of the Federal line. One or two companies of the battered Thirty-seventh Illinois tried to hold back the flood of Confederates with muskets and Colt revolving rifles; some of Davidson's guns fired into the oncoming crowd, while other crews frantically tried to hitch the horses to draw some of the guns off; and Colonel Davis, caught in the middle of the melee, had to flee for his life. The Thirty-seventh Illinois men fell back and Davidson managed to get away with four of his guns, but the Arkansas troops swarmed over the other two. For the moment, they were victorious, but unless they were supported strongly, it would be short-lived.

The Confederates' celebration around the captured cannons was brief. Davidson stopped his four surviving pieces one hundred yards or so down the road and swung them back to fire canister at his old position, but more ominous was what was happening out in Oberson's Field. Even though Peter Osterhaus's artillery had been shelling the woods to the east all along, his line of infantry had remained facing north, in case the Rebels on the other side of the tree line decided to attack along with their comrades in the woods. Now, however, he was swinging the Thirty-sixth Illinois and the Twelfth Missouri around to line up with his artillery and face east toward the woods.

If the Confederates ever had a chance at Leetown, this was it. Hebert and his men had fought their way through Morgan's Woods and punched a hole in the center of the Federal line. Any sort of supporting attack on Osterhaus's position by the Confederate troops on the west side of the Leetown Road might have given Hebert a chance to consolidate his gains and salvage something. Unfortunately, none of the troops in Foster's Field ventured through the four hundred yards of timber to see what was happening on the other side, and no officer was willing to step up and assume command in the absence of other leadership. While Louis Hebert and his four regiments struggled against most of two Federal divisions, five Arkansas, six Texas and two Indian regiments plus three artillery batteries—maybe as many as five thousand men—stood idle only half a mile away.

Within a few minutes, the Confederates were falling back from the captured cannons into the shelter of the woods, where the final act of the drama at Leetown would play out. It was now, as Hebert, McNair and other officers struggled to organize the confusion within their ranks, that Colonel Thomas Pattison's Eighteenth and Twenty-second Indiana launched their attack on the Confederate left, held by the Fourteenth and Fifteenth Arkansas. Louis Hebert had gone over near the Fourteenth Arkansas to try to retrieve several companies of Louisiana men that had wandered there during the confusion and was caught up in the fight.

This part of Davis's plan worked perfectly, at least at first. Pattison's attack came as a complete surprise, and the Arkansas regiments fell back. Some of the Arkansas men ran, but others stood and rallied, and the Federal advance began to get bogged down in the dense brush. In the confusion, smoke and fire, the two Indiana regiments lost contact and drifted apart so that some Confederates moved through the gap and actually ended up behind the Eighteenth Indiana. At this point, however, most of the Arkansas troops

Federal artillery (Peoria Battery) along the east edge of Oberson's Field, facing Morgan's Woods, modern view. *Author's collection.*

were only looking for a way out, and the survivors of both Confederate regiments began to drift to the north, back toward Foster's Field. To make matters worse, a group of senior officers, including Louis Hebert and Colonel Mitchell of the Fourteenth Arkansas, became disoriented in all the smoke and fire and general chaos and wandered away from the battle, lost in the underbrush.

At about this same time, to the west along the road, a puzzling episode took place. During the melee around Davidson's battery, a battalion of the Fourth Missouri Federal cavalry arrived on the scene, commanded by an obviously nervous Major Emeric Meszoros. As the Confederates were falling back into the woods, Colonel Davis decided, for whatever reason, to send the cavalrymen after them. Major Meszoros gave the order but stayed behind while his 250 or so troopers went pounding down the road. They rode right across the face of the Thirty-seventh Illinois and Davidson's guns, forcing them to cease fire, and on up to the Confederates, who hid behind trees and opened fire. Lieutenant William A. Burns later said that, never having been in combat before, he did not at first realize that the sounds he heard were bullets zinging past him. "Once I did realize it," he said, "I thought how pleasant a furlough would be just now!"[101] The ill-conceived cavalry charge quickly fell apart, with the green Missouri troopers scattering in all directions.

The charge of the Fourth Missouri and Pattison's attack from the east effectively ended the Battle of Morgan's Woods. The Confederates were now literally staggering from fatigue, their units hopelessly mingled, and most of their senior officers were either dead, wounded or missing. The Third Louisiana was now leaderless, Colonel Hebert being lost and Major Tunnard having collapsed from exhaustion. One frustrated Louisiana junior officer was heard to say, echoing Wellington at Waterloo, "Would to God it was night or reinforcements would come!"

On the east, the Fourteenth and Fifteenth Arkansas were already streaming back north. Near the Leetown Road, Colonel Evander McNair of the Fourth Arkansas was the senior officer still standing. Seeing Osterhaus's troops in a solid line across Oberson's Field, he decided that he and his troops had done all they could and began to lead the men around him north as well. The Eighteenth and Twenty-second Indiana took a few minutes to realign—Lieutenant Colonel John Hendricks of the Twenty-second had been killed—and then continued their sweep toward Leetown Road but met no resistance. The Confederates were gone. Although no one knew it quite yet, the Battle of Pea Ridge was half won.

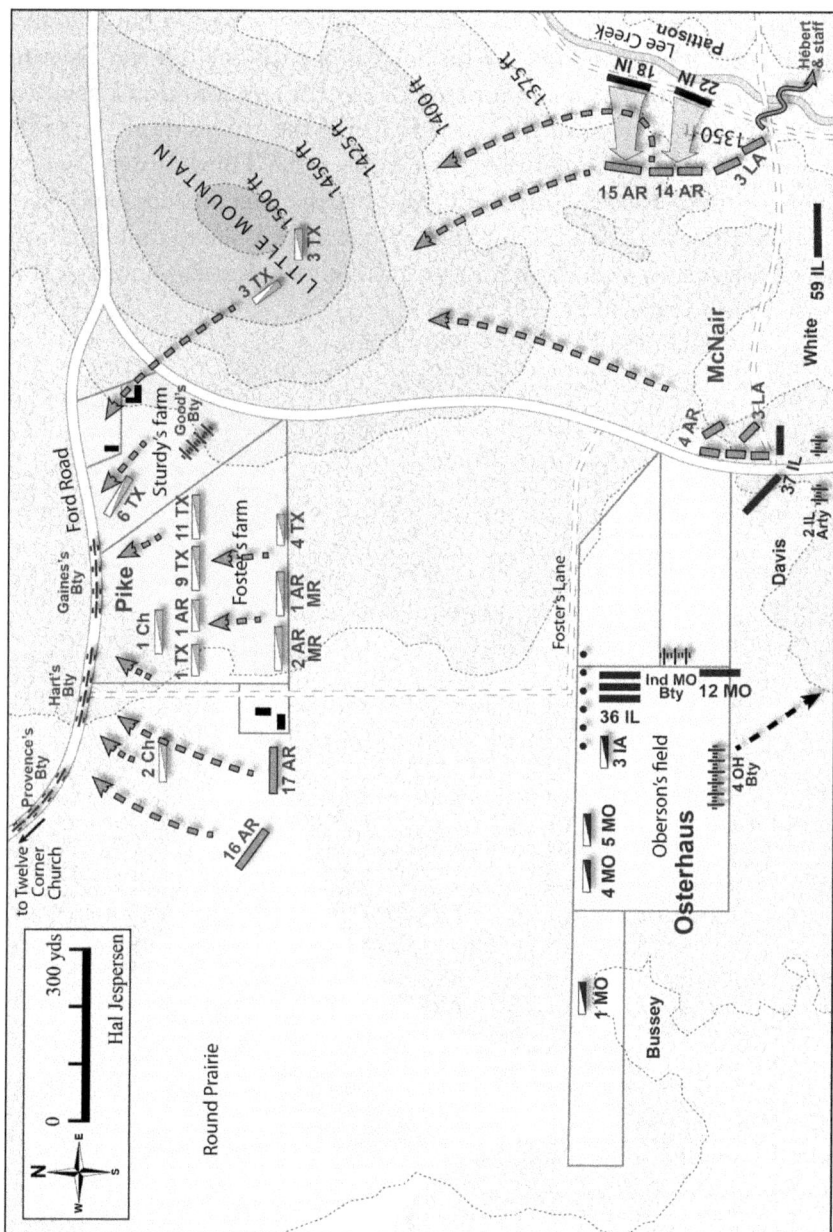

Leetown, 3:00 p.m. to 6:00 p.m. on March 7. Confederates fall back. *Courtesy of Hal Jespersen.*

As the survivors of Morgan's Woods began to arrive back at Foster's Field, McCulloch's once proud division began to fragment. A large part would follow General Albert Pike, who was not part of the division but was the ranking officer left on the field, as he led them back around the Detour to join Price and Van Dorn the next morning. Others would fall back to Camp Stevens, where General Green sat guarding the army's trains, and still others would stay with Colonel Elkanah Greer of the Third Texas Cavalry in the fields north of Foster's farm until 1:30 a.m. the next morning and then march to join Price and Van Dorn.[102] Except for a few isolated units, half of Earl Van Dorn's army was finished. Around Elkhorn Tavern, however, the battle was far from over.

Chapter 15

Elkhorn Tavern

1:00 p.m. to 3:00 p.m.

By the time William Vandever arrived at Elkhorn Tavern, Eugene Carr had pulled his battered First Iowa gunners back up the hill, and the Third Iowa Battery had taken up the artillery duel. What was left of the First Iowa Battery was sent to the rear to repair the damage and resupply with ammunition. Colonel Carr was pretty battered himself. Wounded three times but still on his feet, he quickly briefed Colonel Vandever and sent him and his brigade to the west of the tavern and around the base of Big Mountain to deal with the body of Confederate troops known to be massing there. A little while earlier, the rest of the Third Illinois Cavalry had arrived. Two of its three battalions were already on the right with Colonel Dodge and had helped him drive back the Confederates' first attempt to get around the brigade's right flank. This last battalion was sent to the northwest, where Major Weston's little Twenty-fourth Missouri was holding the left flank. They rounded the base of Big Mountain and made contact with Major Weston but then continued on—presumably searching for the enemy.

So far, the Illinois cavalrymen had been up on the higher ground, but soon they started down a rocky slope where they ran into the front lines of Colonel William Slack's Confederate Second Missouri Brigade. There was a sharp but brief exchange before the surprised Yankee horsemen could scramble back up the hill. This little episode resulted in a few unnecessary casualties for the Illinois riders and gave Slack's Confederates the false impression that they had turned back some large-scale attack, but most of all, it caused the Confederates to delay any movement of their own a little longer, giving the Federals the most precious thing of all: a little more time.[103]

William Vandever's two regiments, the Twenty-fifth Missouri and the Ninth Iowa, deployed between the Tavern and the base of Big Mountain as the rather shaken battalion of the Third Illinois Cavalry fell back past them to take a position on Ford's Farm. Their experience eliminated any doubt about the enemy presence west of the road, so the men of Vandever's brigade dropped their packs and stripped for action. Weston's small Twenty-fourth Missouri was moved to the left and deployed across the high ground on Big Mountain, essentially as skirmishers on that side, while the main body pushed ahead.

The Confederates had held their position after the cavalry retired, and that is where Vandever's men found them—on the sloping ground going down into Tanyard Ravine. The first clash was between skirmishers from both sides, but it cost the Confederates their commander. Colonel Slack had gone forward after the cavalry encounter and was caught in the first volley. He was wounded in the abdomen and taken to the rear, and the command passed to Colonel Thomas Rosser.[104] Ironically, two miles away, Generals McCulloch and McIntosh were falling about the same time.

In this case, holding the higher ground worked against the Federals. The footing was treacherous coming down the slope, and being higher up caused the Yankees to overshoot their targets. The Confederates, on the other hand, were happy for the Federals to close in to distances where their muskets and shotguns became effective. The Missouri Confederates were impressed with the Federals' training and discipline as they fired and advanced, rank after rank, but it couldn't overcome the Confederates' advantage in numbers and position. Before long, the Yankees fell back to the top of the ravine. A second try some time later went no better, and Vandever finally decided to fall back to more favorable ground near the tavern.[105]

After Vandever's brigade fell back, there came a lull while both sides adjusted their lines and prepared for the Confederates' final push that Colonel Carr knew was coming. The attack on the Second Missouri Brigade caused Price to shift some more troops to the west of Telegraph Road. He ordered Colonel Colton Green's Third Missouri Brigade over to reinforce Slack's Second Brigade, now commanded by Colonel Rosser, as well as part of Little's brigade west of the road. Backed by artillery, this increased the Confederate strength west of Telegraph Road to at least three thousand men against Vandever's barely one thousand.

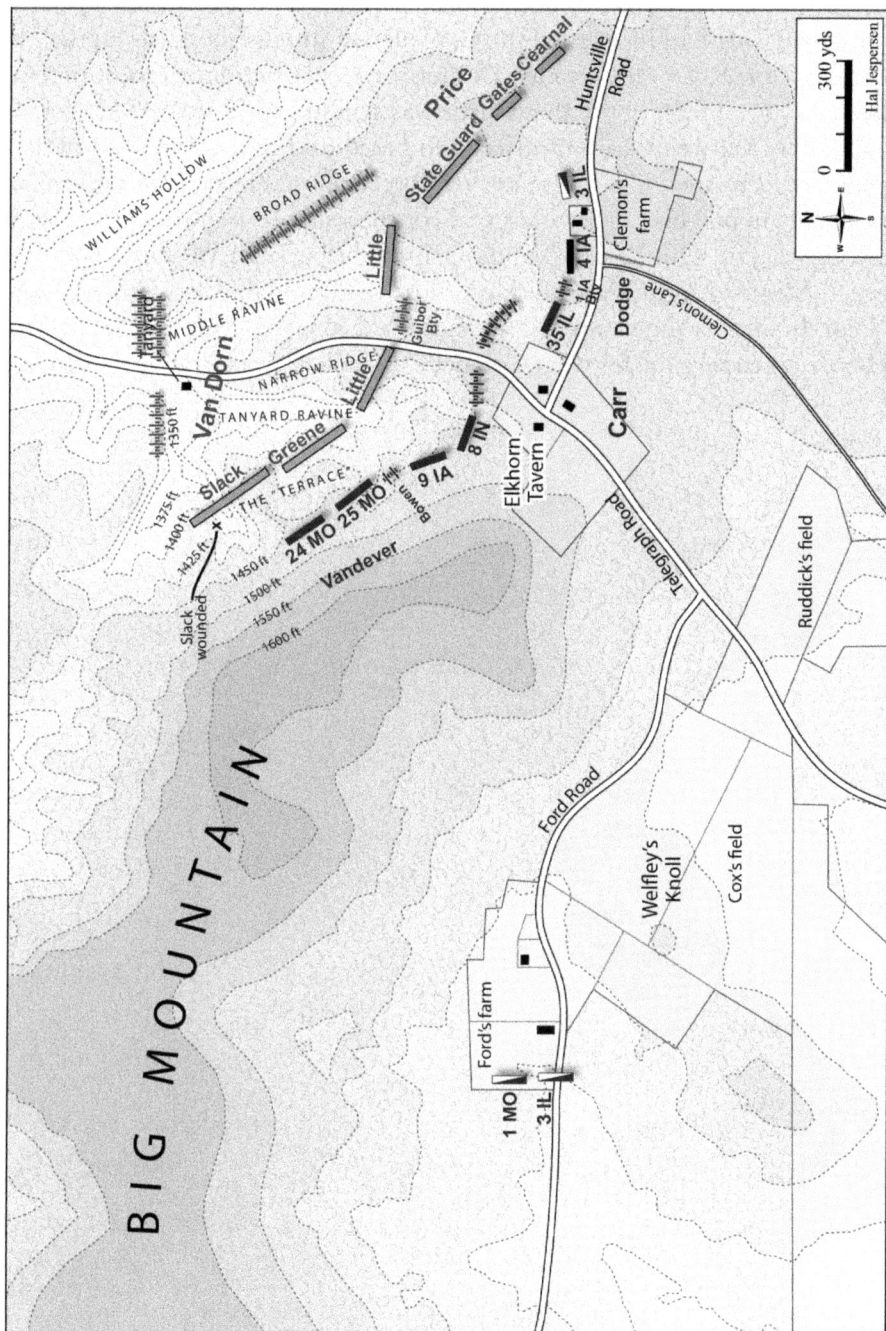

Elkhorn Tavern, 1:00 p.m. to 3:00 p.m. on March 7. Vandever's brigade attacks the Confederate right. *Courtesy of Hal Jespersen.*

Eugene Carr had now tested the Confederate strength both east and west of Telegraph Road and decided to shorten up his own lines, go over to a defensive posture and pray that Curtis was sending more troops very soon. Carr knew full well that he was outnumbered and had no illusions about what would happen if he were not reinforced substantially. He sent orders for Dodge to pull his cavalry back and concentrate between Clemon's Farm and the tavern. On the left, Vandever brought back Eli Weston's Twenty-fourth Missouri in line on his left, added two mountain howitzers under Major Bowen as they arrived and shortened his lines west of the tavern. There now came a lull for what Colonel Carr called "a considerable time."[106]

Chapter 16

Turning an Army Around

When Samuel Curtis began his commanders meeting at 9:00 a.m. on March 7, his army was positioned to meet what he thought was the primary threat. It was dug in along the bluffs on the north bank of Little Sugar Creek, on either side of the Telegraph Road crossing, facing almost due south and probably not extending over a mile. As soon as Major Weston's pickets began reporting and skirmishing with enemy troops, however, Curtis was forced to begin adjusting his lines. By noon, his army had turned to its right and was stretched out in an arc for over four miles, with its left still on Little Sugar Creek but its center now at Leetown with Colonel Osterhaus and its right at Elkhorn Tavern and out the Huntsville Road with Colonel Carr and Colonel Dodge.

When Curtis made his quick visit to Colonel Carr at the tavern, just after noontime, he saw that the army's trains, which were parked just south of the tavern, were in danger from Confederate artillery rounds that were overshooting their targets and beginning to fall among the wagons and teams. His rear area was fast becoming the front lines. Major Weston had already sent his provost wagons, along with the prisoners, back to the area around Pratt's Store, and now it was time to move the supply trains as well. Curtis had no way of knowing, at the time, how fortunate he was. About this time, only a mile away, Colonel Osterhaus was in the process of stopping Ben McCulloch's entire division. Had that not happened, Curtis may have arrived only to see Confederate infantry among his wagons.

The officer whom Curtis tapped for the huge job of moving the army's trains to a safe area was his assistant quartermaster, Captain Byron Carr (the younger brother of Colonel Eugene Carr, at that moment fighting at the tavern). Amid the artillery fire, Captain Carr managed to get the teams in motion and eventually moved the army's supplies, including its rations and reserve ammunition, to the area around Pratt's Store, which would prove crucial the next day.[107] This was no small accomplishment considering that troops and artillery were sharing the same narrow lanes and going in the opposite direction.

In spite of his trip to the tavern to confer with Colonel Carr, Samuel Curtis was forced, for the most part, to follow the progress of the battle by listening from his command post at Pratt's Store. A stream of couriers came and went, giving him reports, but not being able to see for himself was nerve-wracking. Curtis later confided in his brother, "I watched the minute hand of my watch a thousand times." He had been very reluctant to give up the idea that at least some of the Southern army would strike at Little Sugar Creek, but at about 2:00 p.m., another courier came in to report that there was no activity at all in that area. Curtis now decided that it was time to send most of the remaining forces to Carr's aid at the tavern and rode out to the camps on the creek to give General Sigel those orders in person.

Curtis told Sigel to march first to Leetown to see if Osterhaus and Davis had that area under control. If so, he was to proceed on to the tavern as rapidly as possible. Perhaps knowing that Sigel would move very deliberately regardless of his orders, Curtis decided to take a small force under General Asboth directly to the tavern without delay. It was only four companies and a four-gun battery, but Eugene Carr would very soon need anything he could get.

To no one's surprise, Sigel decided to cover all possibilities. He left a small group to guard the camps and sent a second force under Major August Poten up Little Sugar Creek to make sure that no enemy lurked there. A third group, under Captain John Russell, would sweep the woods between the camps and Leetown for stragglers, and the largest group would go with Sigel directly to Leetown. All of this was underway by 4:00 p.m. Major Poten would find no enemy forces until he came near Camp Stevens, where General Martin Green was guarding the Confederate supply wagons. After a short skirmish, Poten would fall back, having learned what he had come for—that there was no threat from that direction. Captain Russell and his men captured about thirty

Brigadier General Franz Sigel, commander of the Federal First and Second Divisions. He commanded the Federal left on March 8. *Courtesy of the Library of Congress.*

Confederates in the woods south of Leetown, including Colonel Louis Hebert and Colonel William Mitchell, who had become lost in the underbrush during the final fighting in Morgan's Woods.[108] Franz Sigel arrived in Oberson's Field at about 5:00 p.m. to find that the battle was over. After carefully sweeping north and picking up some stragglers, he moved on along Ford Road, into the fields south of the tavern, but it was too late to help Carr's division.

Although it wasn't planned—Curtis just reacted to events as they unfolded—what he and the Federal army managed to do on March 7 was remarkable. Over the course of about eight hours, while engaged in two separate battles, they had reversed the entire army, and the supply train had been moved to safety. By the morning of the next day, the rear area had become the front line. The army had been moved back two and a half miles and turned almost two hundred degrees and was now facing northeast.

Chapter 17

The Storm Breaks at Clemon's Farm

The longer the lull in the fighting lasted near the tavern, the more convinced Eugene Carr became that the Confederates were preparing to finally launch a coordinated attack all along his front. Continued pleas for reinforcements had so far resulted in the arrival of welcome but small and piecemeal units. Lieutenant Colonel David Shunk had arrived with five companies of the Eighth Indiana, and five more artillery pieces had been positioned on the left and center, but Carr was still outnumbered almost two to one, with the Confederates having an even bigger advantage in artillery.

Sometime earlier, across from Carr's position at the tavern, Earl Van Dorn and Sterling Price were conferring when a courier arrived with the news that McCulloch's division had stopped and was fighting north of Leetown. The courier also reported that he had come around the Detour because Ford Road east of Little Mountain was blocked by Federal cavalry. This told Van Dorn that the support he was expecting from that direction would not arrive anytime soon if at all. A little later, Major "Sul" Ross of the Sixth Texas Cavalry would arrive with word that both McCulloch and McIntosh were dead and that their division was essentially leaderless.[109] To make matters worse, at about this time General Price was wounded, hit by a rifle ball in his right arm.

As Price's staff was attending to his injured arm—Price refused to leave the field—Earl Van Dorn decided to order the general attack that he had been planning, even though there would now be no help from McCulloch. Couriers went out with orders, and the Confederate units began to attempt to align across the uneven ground and underbrush. As this was happening, Carr was shortening his line, and before long, this movement was observed.

Colonel Elijah Gates's First Missouri Cavalry had been on the Confederate left most of the day, scouting and sparring with Dodge's Illinois riders. He now sent a rider to Van Dorn reporting that, with the shortening of the line on the Federal right, Dodge's position near Clemon's Farm could be easily turned. With this information, Van Dorn decided to revise his original plan. The assault on the right—toward the tavern—would go as planned, but not until the Missouri State Guard troops on the left pulled back and moved farther to their left. From there they could advance under the cover of Williams Hollow to the Huntsville Road and then turn on Dodge, rolling up the Federal right, while Henry Little and Tom Rosser's men attacked Carr and Vandever at the Tavern. All of this, of course, took even more time.[110]

By 4:00 p.m., riders from the Third Illinois Cavalry had discovered the Confederate movement and informed Dodge that the enemy was across the Huntsville Road. There was nothing the Iowa colonel could do but deploy to meet them. To do this, Dodge moved the Fourth Iowa off the Huntsville Road and put it in position facing Price's Confederates along a lane that ran down the western edge of Mr. Clemon's cornfield. As luck would have it, Mr. Clemon had been cleaning up that part of his property, and a lot of dead trees and limbs were piled up along that western fence line. In the next half hour, the Fourth Iowa used them to throw up the only fieldworks erected by any unit at Pea Ridge, and the men finished just in time.

At about 4:30 p.m., the long-anticipated Confederate attack began. Sterling Price, wounded arm and all, had managed to coax almost two thousand exhausted men and horses pulling eleven guns up Williams Hollow onto the Pea Ridge plateau and now opened fire with his artillery. This was the signal that the Confederate troops along Telegraph Road were waiting for, and Henry Little, Colton Green and Tom Rosser's men began to move up the road and climb out of the ravines to face the Federals at the tavern. Price's troops had things their own way for a while, with only the riders of the Third Illinois skirmishing and falling back before them. Then they reached the eastern edge of Clemon's Field and things changed. Across the small cornfield waited the Fourth Iowa behind its impromptu fortifications.

At Clemon's Field, the Third Illinois troopers fell back to Clemon's Lane on Dodge's right flank, and Price set up his artillery across the field. Due to a crown in the middle of the field, the Confederate shells would tend to fly high, but for the next half hour, Colonel Dodge and the men simply kept their heads down and became as small as possible while

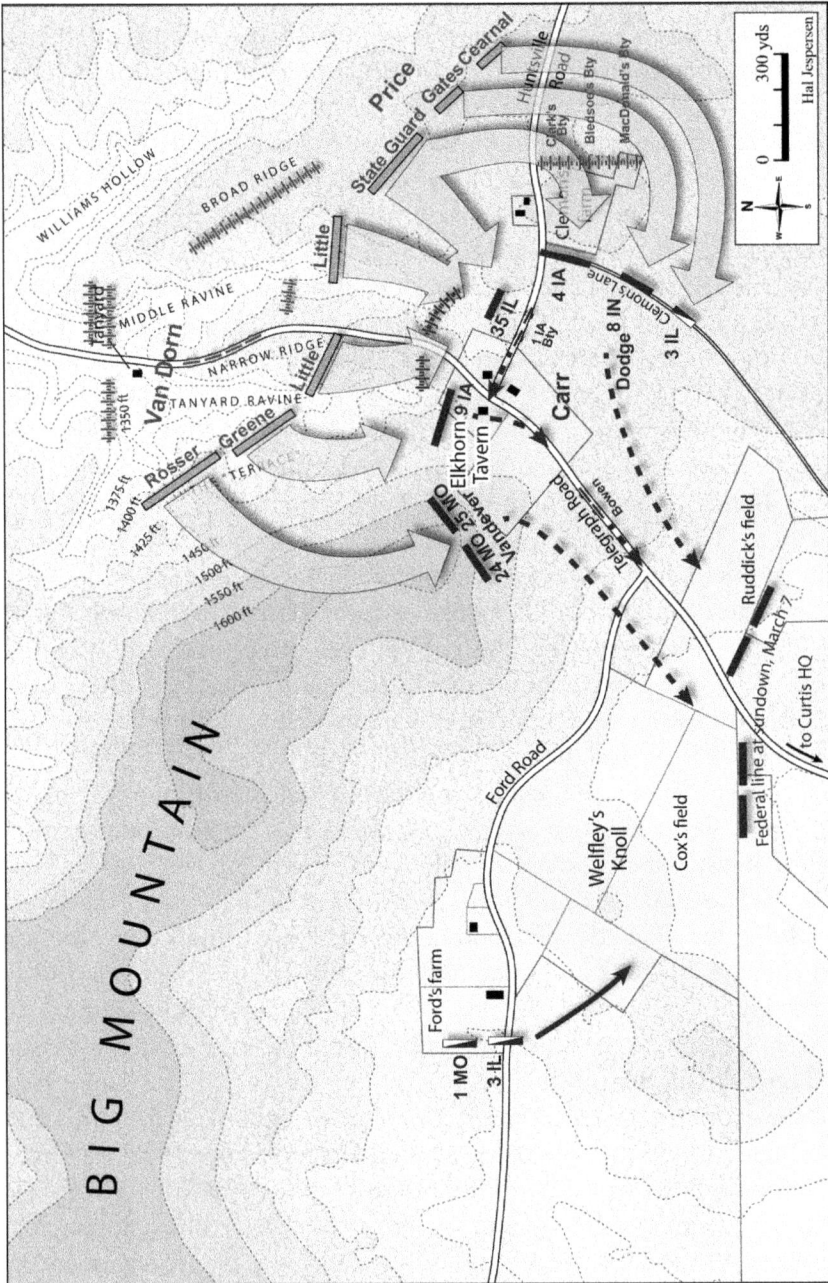

Elkhorn Tavern, 4:30 p.m. to sundown on March 7. Van Dorn and Price attack. *Courtesy of Hal Jespersen.*

the eleven Rebel guns blasted their makeshift breastworks from only two hundred yards away.

The trees all around them were shredded by a steel hurricane, but thanks to their preparations, the Iowa men were relatively untouched. When Price finally sent his first unit across the field, they were ready, and Colonel John B. Clark's small five-hundred-man Third State Guard Division was handled quite roughly. Within a few minutes, they were streaming back across the field in disorder. Another round of artillery fire commenced, and then, unbelievably, Clark and his men re-formed and came again, still unsupported, with even more tragic results. As they fell back for a second time, the Confederates heard the Iowa men cheering.

Following the disaster with Clark's two attacks, Price now began moving around both flanks, trying to cut off the Fourth Iowa. Dodge had the Thirty-fifth Illinois on his left but only a few dismounted cavalry on his right, so he sent to Carr at the tavern for help. Hard-pressed himself now at the tavern, Carr still agreed to send the few companies of the recently arrived Eighth Indiana, and they fell in to help the cavalrymen on Dodge's right. So far, his line had held, but it was only a matter of time.

Chapter 18

The Storm Breaks at Elkhorn Tavern

As Colonel Dodge and his men were trying to hold back Price's State Guard, the Confederates along Telegraph Road and to the west near the foot of Big Mountain began their assault. Earl Van Dorn was commanding this part of the field personally, while Price commanded the State Guard troops facing the Federal right. Unlike Price's men, who were finally on level ground, most of Van Dorn's men still had to climb up out of Tanyard Ravine to get at the Yankees holding the ground around the tavern. With so much firing already done there, a pall of smoke hung in the low ground, masking the Confederates' approach. One of the Ninth Iowa men, waiting to the west of the tavern, remembered the Confederates finally coming in sight through the smoke. He said that one moment there was nothing, and in the next, the slope in front of him was covered with Rebels.[111]

Like Dodge's men in Clemon's Field, Carr and Vandever's men near the tavern were contesting every yard but were soon hard-pressed. Henry Little's brigade came up both sides of Telegraph Road and began to threaten the Federal artillery near the tavern plus the battered Thirty-fifth Illinois, which was already fighting a State Guard unit on its right. West of the tavern, Colton Green and Tom Rosser's brigades were slugging it out with William Vandever's Ninth Iowa and two Missouri regiments. One of the Ninth Iowa officers later wrote, "I charged the battlements at Vicksburg…and assisted in driving the Confederates from their almost impregnable position on Missionary Ridge…but in all my army experience, I did not see any fighting compared with the plain open field conflict that occurred in and around the Elkhorn Tavern on March 7, 1862."[112]

Since Tom Rosser's men (Slack's old brigade) were on the western end of the Confederate line, Van Dorn ordered him to sweep around and try to flank Vandever's line. It was after 5:00 p.m. before the exhausted men could make the climb and get in position, and by that time, Vandever had faced the Twenty-fourth and Twenty-fifth Missouri to the left to meet them— Missouri loyalists facing Missouri Rebels. Vandever's line was now bent back in a shallow arc as more and more Confederates emerged onto the more level ground. As Rosser's men assaulted the Federal left, Henry Little's First Brigade approached the tavern. Since Carr had sent the Eighth Indiana to Dodge, the only troops there to meet them were the right-hand companies of the Ninth Iowa and some artillery.

Captain Mortimer Hayden still had three guns of his Third Iowa Battery in action near the tavern,

Colonel William Vandever, commander of the Federal Second Brigade, Fourth Division, under Eugene Carr. Fought the Confederate troops west of Elkhorn Tavern on March 7. *Courtesy of the Library of Congress.*

and together with the Ninth Iowa's small-arms fire, they punished Little's First Brigade as they came up Telegraph Road, but Little's men would not be denied. As the Confederates came on with a yell, the Ninth Iowa fell back, and Hayden only got away with one of his three guns. Grenville Dodge and his men were still hanging on at Clemon's Field, but the trap was closing around Elkhorn Tavern.

Eugene Carr had held his position all afternoon, but when he saw his line near the tavern come apart, he knew that it was time to go. He told

Reconstruction of Elkhorn Tavern at Pea Ridge National Military Park. *Author's collection.*

William Vandever to save what he could of his brigade and fall back to a band of trees several hundred yards in the rear. Each regiment managed to make its own way back, and they formed a new line along a fence at the edge of the trees. Fortunately for Carr, the Confederates were not able to follow up immediately.

Having driven off the Federals, confusion prevailed with the Rebels near the tavern. Units were mingled and, in several cases, fired on friendly troops who were partially obscured by the smoke that lingered on the field. Some of the famished Missouri troops stopped to feast on army rations they found and plundered a sutler's store. Within a few minutes, however, some groups were following the retreating Yankees, while others milled around near the tavern.

Several hundred yards east of the tavern, Colonel Dodge still held his position, but his ammunition was running very low. When word came that Colonel Carr had fallen back from the tavern, Dodge had his men fire one last volley and then brought them off through the trees into Ruddick's Field in good order, bringing all their wounded with them.[113] On Dodge's left, the battered Thirty-fifth Illinois fell back as best it could, but Colonel William P. Chandler and about forty men were surrounded and captured.[114]

By now, Carr and Vandever's men were also falling back again. They had held for a few minutes at their new position, but as one of Carr's officers put it, "the ammunition was about exhausted and so were we." During this second retreat, Lieutenant Colonel Francis Herron, who had commanded the Ninth Iowa all day, was wounded and captured when his horse was killed and he was trapped beneath it.[115] As Carr's men fell back out of the band of trees into Ruddick's Field, however, they saw a collection of artillery. These were guns that had either escaped the Confederate break through or had fallen back earlier to refill their ammunition chests and then returned to the field. They were from several different batteries and were waiting for new orders.

Lieutenant Colonel Francis J. Herron, commander of the Ninth Iowa in Vandever's brigade. Herron was wounded and captured on March 7. *Courtesy of the Library of Congress.*

Using these batteries, Carr and Vandever's survivors cobbled together one last line across Telegraph Road near the south edge of Ruddick's Field, just in time. Out of the woods they had just vacated came a large mass of Rebels in hot pursuit. With their blood up, the Confederates ignored orders from their officers to stop and align their ranks and started across the field more as a mob than an army. If they thought the Yankees were finished, however, they were badly mistaken. Thirteen guns firing canister and the rifles of Vandever's brigade tore them apart. Some of them almost reached the Federal guns but finally broke and fell back to the tree line. Carr's last line had held.

At about this time, a few minutes before sundown, General Curtis and General Asboth arrived with five hundred fresh troops and eight more guns. These men added to Carr's somewhat ragged line, as did Dodge's men who came into the field to their right. General Samuel Curtis, thirty years after West Point, was now about to personally lead men in battle for the first time.

Having just arrived on the field, Curtis was confident that, with this makeshift force, he could drive the Confederates back and retake the lost ground. With that in mind, he opened with his artillery and then ordered the infantry to move forward. When Colonel Dodge informed Curtis that his Fourth Iowa had been fighting all afternoon and now had no ammunition, he was told to fix bayonets and have his men move forward anyway, which they did. Curtis's counterattack made headway for a while, but the Confederates began to push back as he approached the intersection of Ford and Telegraph Roads. Since it was almost dark, Curtis wisely decided to fall back to the southern edge of Ruddick's Field for the night. During the attack, General Asboth was wounded, but Curtis came through his first combat unhurt.

Brigadier General Alexander S. Asboth, commander of the Federal Second Division under Franz Sigel. Wounded bringing reinforcements to Elkhorn Tavern on March 7. *Courtesy of the Massachusetts Commandery, (MOLLUS).*

Artillery exchanges continued for another hour or so, lighting the battlefield with brilliant flashes, but in the end, the two armies were content to stay where they were. On the north, Confederate officers struggled to bring some order to their units, while the men wandered the rear areas, searching for something to eat. To the south, the Yankees were generally in better shape and were forming a line roughly even with the southern edge of Ruddick's Field, while the Confederates held the northern edge. Both armies were settling in for the night, separated in some places by three hundred yards or less.[116]

Earl Van Dorn had managed to put at least part of his army across the Federal supply line and had finally taken the area around Elkhorn Tavern, but he hadn't won yet. Samuel Curtis's line at the tavern had finally been routed and pushed back half a mile, but he hadn't lost. What each commander and each army was able to do during the coming night would decide the winner tomorrow.

Chapter 19

The Night of March 7–8

As the night came on and the artillery firing died away, both sides began the sad process of finding and caring for the wounded. In this sparsely settled area, practically every building or hut was pressed into service. Behind the Confederate lines, Elkhorn Tavern was used as a hospital, with over one hundred men housed in the tavern and in the yard and outbuildings. On the Federal side, the wounded were brought to the few buildings around Pratt's Store and Leetown, and tents were pitched to accommodate the overflow. Surgeons on both sides operated by the light of lamps and candles, trying to staunch bleeding, probing for bullets and amputating limbs in the most primitive of conditions. A Federal surgeon said, "Our preparations were wholly inadequate." Conditions on the Confederate side were even worse.[117]

As they searched in the darkness through the underbrush for the wounded, soldiers often found themselves working alongside the same men they had recently been trying to kill. Dr. Washington L. Grammage, surgeon of the Fourth Arkansas, established his regimental hospital north of the battlefield at Leetown and told of going out after dark to find some of his wounded troops: "[W]hen my ambulance came up, I called for volunteers to go with me to hunt up the wounded…When we got to the edge of the timber, I met a Federal ambulance which I hailed…They told me they were hunting for wounded men: I answered that my business was the same, and we went back to the field together."[118]

While doctors and orderlies cared for the wounded, other men tried to find their units, get something to eat or just find a fire to warm themselves.

Food and water were particularly critical on the Confederate side, where many men had eaten nothing for thirty-six hours or more. That night, some were lucky, but many were not. Asa Payne, of the Third Missouri Regiment of Henry Little's First Brigade, was luckier than most. He had passed by Elkhorn Tavern during the Confederate attack and managed to fill his haversack from the sutler's store he found inside. Later, as he and the men of the First Brigade lay along the northern side of Ruddick's Field, he said, "I feasted on sardines and cheese that I got passing through the sutler's store, and I imagined that I could taste them at intervals for many years afterwards."[119]

During the night, units on both sides continued to move around, getting in position for tomorrow's fight. On the Federal side, General Sigel had taken his men, first to Leetown and Oberson's Field and then over the saddle near Little Mountain to camp near Ford's Farm after dark. Later, he decided to take them back to the camps on Little Sugar Creek for rations but was stopped by his commander near Pratt's Store. Curtis was afraid that Sigel's men would be late returning to the battlefield, so he told Sigel to keep them there and do what the other units near the front were doing—sending small groups from each company back to their camps for provisions.

During the night, Colonel Davis's Third Division, which had born the brunt of the fighting at Leetown, was put in position astride Telegraph Road, tying in with Carr's battered Fourth Division, which was on its right. Franz Sigel's half of the Federal army would begin to arrive after sunrise, with Peter Osterhaus's First Division on Colonel Davis's left and General Asboth's Second Division extending the line west across Cox's Field.

Across from the Federal line, General Price's State Guard units faced Carr and Davis's men across Ruddick's Field, while Henry Little's First Missouri Brigade extended the line west of Telegraph Road. On Henry Little's right, Tom Rosser had the Second Missouri Brigade bent back at an angle, with his right in the rocks at the base of Big Mountain and some of Pike's Cherokees on the high ground atop the ridge. Most of the Confederate artillery was massed behind the lines near Elkhorn Tavern. During the night, several units from McCulloch's scattered division, led by General Albert Pike, arrived. The Sixteenth Arkansas was put on Little's left, and Seventeenth Arkansas and the First Arkansas Mounted Rifles were put on either side of Telegraph Road, behind Henry Little's First Brigade. The group led by Colonel Elkanah Greer of the Third Texas Cavalry would not arrive until almost dawn.

In addition to sending small groups back for food and blankets, the Federal units that had been engaged during the day were also able to replenish their cartridge boxes from the reserve supplies near Pratt's Store, and the artillery batteries were able to refill their ammunition chests. On the Confederate side, this was not the case. The Federal supply trains were within a mile of their new line, which allowed all of the Federal troops and artillery batteries to go into the battle on March 8 with full ammunition loads. The Confederate supply wagons, on the other hand, were far out of position. Most likely, with all the rush to get behind the Federal army and the fighting on March 7, Van Dorn and Price had simply lost track of his supply train, far in the rear, and assumed that it would follow.

At the beginning of the march from the Boston Mountains, General Martin Green's small State Guard division was ordered to bring up the rear of the column and guard the army's trains, which it had done. As the army neared Camp Stevens on March 6, the column had become so strung out that Green and the trains were miles behind, and it was after daylight on March 7 before they reached Camp Stevens. Green, in his official report, said that he was then ordered to leave the baggage in camp and defend a crossroads to the northeast, where he and some other troops remained all day. A Federal report, however, noted that Confederate supply wagons were seen on the Bentonville Detour near Twelve Corner Church about noontime but were headed back toward Camp Stevens. Whether Green started the trains toward Van Dorn's army on March 7 and turned back for some reason, which seems most likely, or stayed near Camp Stevens all day, which he claimed in his report, it is clear that the Confederate trains, with all their reserve ammunition, were near Camp Stevens at sundown. Unfortunately for the Confederates, Green neglected to report his position to either General Price, his immediate superior, or to General Van Dorn.[120]

Somehow, in all the action of March 7, General Van Dorn and General Price had lost track of the supply train but, hearing nothing from General Green, believed that it had come up during the day and was close at hand. Accordingly, sometime before sunup on March 8, General Price sent a messenger to find the trains and bring up the ammunition wagons. About the same time, eight miles away, General Green finally decided to communicate his situation to his commander and sent a messenger of his own from Camp Stevens to find General Price and ask for orders. The two messengers must have passed each other on the Bentonville Detour, because not long after his courier left, Green received Price's order to bring up the trains and got them on the road as soon as possible.

Elkhorn Tavern, Federal and Confederate positions at 8:00 a.m. on March 8. *Courtesy of Hal Jespersen.*

Earl Van Dorn probably did not find out until the battle was already joined on March 8 that he was separated from his ammunition wagons by almost eight miles, with most of the Federal army in between. Van Dorn would later blame an unnamed—and probably fictitious—ordnance officer "who could not find his wagons" for the coming disaster, but as commanding general, the responsibility was his.

As the sun rose on March 8, Earl Van Dorn and the Confederate army faced a new reality. Yesterday, they had faced one of Curtis's divisions and outnumbered them almost two to one. Today they faced all four Federal divisions, drawn up in a line almost a mile long, and were now on the short end of the odds.

Chapter 20

A Continual Thunder

I f the Federal army was finally united on the morning of March 8, the various outlooks of its senior commanders were not. General Curtis made his dispositions and was confident that he could defeat the Confederates in the coming fight, but as the night wore on, Alexander Asboth became more convinced that they were surrounded and must cut their way out back into Missouri or be captured. By morning, Asboth had brought his friend Franz Sigel around to his point of view so that, although they both fought well, they believed that they were punching a hole in the enemy line so the army could escape. Samuel Curtis, however, had no thought of escape. He intended to win.[121]

As the sun came up on March 8, the two armies began to stir. Smoke and haze still hung on parts of the battlefield, and frost was on the grass from the cold night. The Federal Third and Fourth Divisions were beginning to move around at the edge of the timber on the south edge of Ruddick's Field and were watching the Confederates doing the same about three hundred yards across the way. Colonel Peter Osterhaus and an aide had earlier completed a reconnaissance across Cox's Field toward Ford's Farm and were bringing the first regiment of his division (the Forty-fourth Illinois) forward from Pratt's Store when cannon fire began at the front. Colonel Davis had ordered a battery to open fire on the opposite tree line, which caused the Confederate infantry to fall back but also triggered a return barrage from some masked Rebel batteries that sent the Federals scrambling back as well. At one point, some Arkansas and Missouri men started across Ruddick's Field to threaten the Federal line but were turned back by Yankee artillery.

The early morning artillery duel caused a lot of excitement at Federal headquarters at Pratt's Store and encouraged the rest of Sigel's troops to cut short their breakfast and hurry up Telegraph Road, followed by General Curtis himself. By the time the rest of the First and Second Divisions arrived, the artillery fire had died away, and by about 8:00 a.m., the Federal line was in place (as shown on the map on page 120). By then, the smoke and haze had dissipated, and Earl Van Dorn's men got their first good look at the enemy.[122]

Franz Sigel's performance up to now had been mixed at best, with most of his troop movements slow and deliberate. His most inspired action was, in fact, his retreat from Bentonville on March 6. This morning, however, commanding the left of the Federal line, he was superb. Once his First and Second Divisions were in place, he began to move his batteries forward toward the Confederate line and toward a spot of high ground to his left near Ford's Farm that Colonel Osterhaus had found earlier that morning. His infantry followed, and the Federal line west of Telegraph Road began to swing forward to line up with the Third and Fourth Divisions on their right. Van Dorn countered by sending Captain John Good's Texas battery onto the field in front of Henry Little's line with orders to break up the Federal formation. Here Captain Good unlimbered his six guns and opened fire. To Good's left, near Telegraph Road, Captain William Wade's Missouri battery soon joined in.

When the Rebel guns opened on them, the Federal infantry went to the ground. The Yankees had the advantage of higher ground, so the Confederate fire often flew over them and caused very few casualties. Sigel now wheeled forward parts of six batteries of his own totaling twenty-one guns, and the largest artillery duel ever seen on the continent up to that time got underway in earnest. On the left of his line, Sigel sent Captain Martin Welfley's Missouri Independent battery to the little hill that Colonel Osterhaus had discovered. It turned out to be the best artillery position on the entire field, and several other batteries joined him. Today it is known as "Welfley's Knoll."

Franz Sigel went from battery to battery, personally directing the sighting of some of the guns and encouraging the crews, and the Federal fire became much more accurate and effective than the few Confederate guns could match. Captain Good later wrote his wife, "We were no more in position than three batteries opened a perfect storm of round and shrapnell shot and shell. We fought all for three quarters of an hour. Our shell and shrapnell having been expended and twenty-five men killed, wounded, and missing, I ordered the battery to retire."[123]

Behind Captain Good's and Captain Wade's batteries, Henry Little's First Brigade could only huddle in the tree line and try to find some shelter from the shot and shell that fell around them. Limbs and sometimes whole trees came crashing down as the Federal guns pounded the batteries just in front of them.

Captain Good's battery fought until their ammunition gave out and then fell back. Before long, Captain Wade did the same. Once they got in position along the high ground in Cox's Field, the Federal artillery was simply devastating. Seeing Good's battery coming back, Van Dorn ordered Hart's Arkansas battery to replace them. John Good said that Hart was cut to pieces in ten minutes and retired. To Van Dorn, however, it looked more like cowardice. He ordered Hart arrested and his battery's ammunition given to Captain Churchill Clark's Missouri battery that was coming up to replace them. Clark was only nineteen years old, but he and his battery were already well known for their bravery under fire. After the experience of Good and Wade, however, Van Dorn ordered Clark to stay out of the open field and set up farther back near the intersection of Telegraph and Ford Road. There they would stubbornly hold their ground until ordered to fall back, and there young Clark would die at his post.

In spite of having fifteen batteries of artillery—most of them around Elkhorn Tavern—Earl Van Dorn never managed to get more than three of them in action against Sigel's line at any one time on March 8. Whether because of low ammunition supplies or poor management on Van Dorn's part, the Federal artillery simply overwhelmed the Confederates that morning, and much of the credit goes to Franz Sigel, who directed it personally. To make matters worse, it was probably about this time—in the middle of the Federal bombardment—that General Price received General Green's message and learned that the ammunition wagons were out of reach at Camp Stevens. When General Van Dorn was told, he was shocked. Because of the heavy fighting the day before, many of the Confederate units had almost exhausted their cartridge boxes and artillery ammunition chests, and without those supply wagons, the army couldn't hold. Green and the wagons were already on their way toward the army—a fact that Van Dorn did not know—but were still too far away. Feeling that he had no choice, Van Dorn sent the messenger back with orders for Green to try to save the trains by taking them back

Elkhorn Tavern, 10:30 a.m. to 12:00 p.m. on March 8. Federal attack and Confederate withdrawal. *Courtesy of Hal Jespersen.*

One of the Confederate artillery positions along Telegraph Road on the morning of March 8 (Wade's Battery). Looking west, with Welfley's Knoll in the distance, modern view. *Author's collection.*

through Bentonville to Elm Springs. Then the Confederate commander began to try and save his army.

Once the three batteries of Captains Good, Wade and Hart had withdrawn, the Confederate fire decreased substantially, with only fire from Captain Clark's battery farther back, as well as some sporadic fire from other batteries around the tavern replying to the Federal guns. Sigel now directed three of his batteries to shift their fire to the left and concentrate on the Confederates near the base of Big Mountain. This was the Second Brigade under Tom Rosser. Sigel would later say in his after-action report:

> His [the enemy's] *infantry was already lodged upon the hill, seeking shelter behind the rocks and stones, whilst some pieces of artillery worked around to gain the plateau. I immediately ordered the two howitzers of the reserve (Second Ohio, under Lieutenant Gransevoort) and the two pieces of Captain Elbert's flying battery to report to Colonel Osterhaus on the left to shell and batter the enemy on the hill. This was done in concert with Hoffmann's battery and with terrible effect to the enemy, as the rocks and stones worked as hard as the shells and shot.* [124]

When the Federal artillery turned their attention to Rosser's brigade, his men who had taken shelter in the rocks and boulders and sandstone columns at the base of Big Mountain found that, instead of a place of safety, the Yankee guns turned it into a deathtrap. Canister and grapeshot ricocheted in all directions, and solid shot produced a shower of deadly stone fragments. As Tom Rosser later said, all the Confederates could do was take it: "Each battalion of the command received a shower of cannon ball and grape for at least an hour without the possibility of discharging a gun. At this time we were ordered to fall back, and in a short time afterwards I received the order to retreat."[125]

By 10:00 a.m., Rosser's Second Missouri Brigade was falling back under orders from General Van Dorn, leaving his right flank open. Rosser's men didn't know it yet, but they were beginning the retreat of the entire army.

In the last two hours, Franz Sigel had conducted one of the few really effective artillery preparations in the Civil War. All the time he was moving and sighting his guns, he was also moving his infantry into position to take advantage of the artillery barrage, and by 10:00 a.m. he had established the First and Second Divisions in a solid line from Telegraph Road to Ford's Farm. For most of this time, General Curtis left Sigel to his work and spent his time east of the road with Colonel Davis and Colonel Carr's Third and Fourth Divisions, moving them up as Sigel's men moved and directing the batteries near him to fire over the tree line into the area around the tavern. Finally, just after 10:00 a.m., Curtis rode across Cox's Field and met with

View to the west from Big Mountain, with Welfley's Knoll to the left, Ford's Farm in the right foreground (with the two trees) and Little Mountain in the distance. *Author's collection.*

Sigel and Osterhaus on Ford's Farm. Reviewing the effect of the artillery on the Confederate line, Curtis and Sigel decided that it was time for the infantry to advance.

Starting on the far left, three Missouri Federal regiments started up the slopes of Big Mountain and flushed the Cherokee riders off the summit. Next, the Thirty-sixth Illinois, which had held Oberson's Field and killed two Confederate generals the day before, moved forward through the area just abandoned by Tom Rosser's Second Brigade. Just to the south, Henry Little's First Missouri Confederate brigade was now in a perilous situation as the Federal Twelfth Missouri swept around its open right flank and the Forty-fourth and Twenty-fifth Illinois came at them head on. If the Yankees thought that two hours lying under that bombardment had softened up the Confederates, however, they were disappointed. Henry Little's men contested every yard, and the fighting in the brush near the junction of Telegraph and Ford Roads was some of the bitterest on the field.[126]

Just before the Federal infantry attacked, Colonel Little received orders from Van Dorn to hold his position as long as possible. Unknown to most of the men at the front, General Van Dorn had already begun the army's retreat. Colonel Rosser's brigade was already passing around the tavern on the way out the Huntsville Road, and several other units and batteries would follow. Henry Little's men were covering their retreat.[127] Across the road to the east, Colonel Davis's Third Division was moving toward the

View to the south from Big Mountain. Pea Ridge Visitor Center and Telegraph Road are in the distance. Ruddick's Field is to the left. Welfley's Knoll is just out of view to the right, and Elkhorn Tavern is just out of view to the left. *Author's collection.*

Sixteenth Arkansas and toward the Missouri State Guard units on the north edge of Ruddick's Field, and these Confederates would soon make a fighting withdrawal toward Clemon's Lane. The charge across Ruddick's Field by Davis's entire Third Division was a sight to behold, and Franz Sigel, watching from across the road, is said to have remarked to an aide in his thick German accent: "Oh! Dot vas lofley!"[128]

All along the line, the Confederates were falling back, but deliberately and in generally good order. As Henry Little's line retreated past Ford Road, they came upon Captain Churchill Clark's battery. It was one of the few Confederate battery still firing at the advancing Yankees, and it was taking a beating from the Federal batteries. As they began to limber up to fall back with the First Brigade, Captain Clark was killed as a solid shot took off his head. A few minutes earlier, Colonel Benjamin Rives, one of Little's regimental commanders, had been mortally wounded nearby.[129]

Unit after unit, Earl Van Dorn's army was falling back, with most marching east out Huntsville Road, but around Elkhorn Tavern, confusion reigned. No senior officer was there to give orders, so each of the Confederate batteries around the tavern retreated as it saw best. Those with any ammunition left fired parting shots at the Federals advancing toward the tavern. Bledsoe's State Guard battery fired its last shells and then loaded its blacksmith tools and spare trace chains to fire a final shot before joining the exodus of Confederate guns escaping north up Telegraph Road.[130] Part of that group going north was Captain John Good's Texas battery. Captain Good would spend the next week hauling his guns almost one hundred miles through the north Arkansas wilderness to bring them safely down to the Arkansas River Valley.

Just before noon, the center of the Federal line reached Elkhorn Tavern. The units on the left had gone up and over Big Mountain and down the other side to Telegraph Road, barely missing the Confederate artillery on its way north. The Third and Fourth Divisions, on the right, stopped on the Huntsville Road near Clemon's Farm. Standing around the tavern, the soldiers were amazed at the damage their artillery barrage had done. Great cheers were raised, and even the normally reserved Samuel Curtis rode among his men, waving his hat and shouting, "Victory!" He later wrote to his brother, "A charge of infantry like that last closing scene has never been made on this continent. It was the most terribly magnificent sight that can be imagined."

All of a sudden, the battle was over, and Curtis and his men had won.[131]

Chapter 21

A Retreat Worse than a Dozen Battles

After the battle was over, the Confederate army was fragmented and retreated in three different directions. From the area around Elkhorn Tavern, troops streamed north on Telegraph Road toward Missouri. Many of these were artillery units that were joined by some infantry companies that had gotten separated from their regiments plus the entire Seventeenth Arkansas, which had evidently missed the turn onto the Huntsville Road. Swept along with this flood was General Albert Pike, who tried in vain to get some of the units to rally, but a few well-timed Federal artillery rounds fired down the road put an end to that, and the tide moved farther north. Within a couple of miles, this group began to fragment as well. Captain John Good's Texas battery and some others turned off the road to the east, hoping to somehow make their way back south to rejoin the main body. Hundreds of others—including Pike—turned west on the Bentonville Detour, back the way they had come thirty-six hours earlier. The rest kept heading north back into Missouri.

A second group was led by General Martin Green, the commander of the supply train. Upon receiving General Price's order to bring up the supply train, General Green had put the wagons on the Bentonville Detour and was plodding along toward Telegraph Road as fast as the worn-out teams could pull. General Green's command had more than doubled in the last twenty-four hours. Two new regiments had followed in the wake of the army up from the Boston Mountains but had stopped when they reached Camp Stevens and joined Green's detachment.[132] After the battle at Leetown, several units from McCulloch's division drifted back toward Camp Stevens

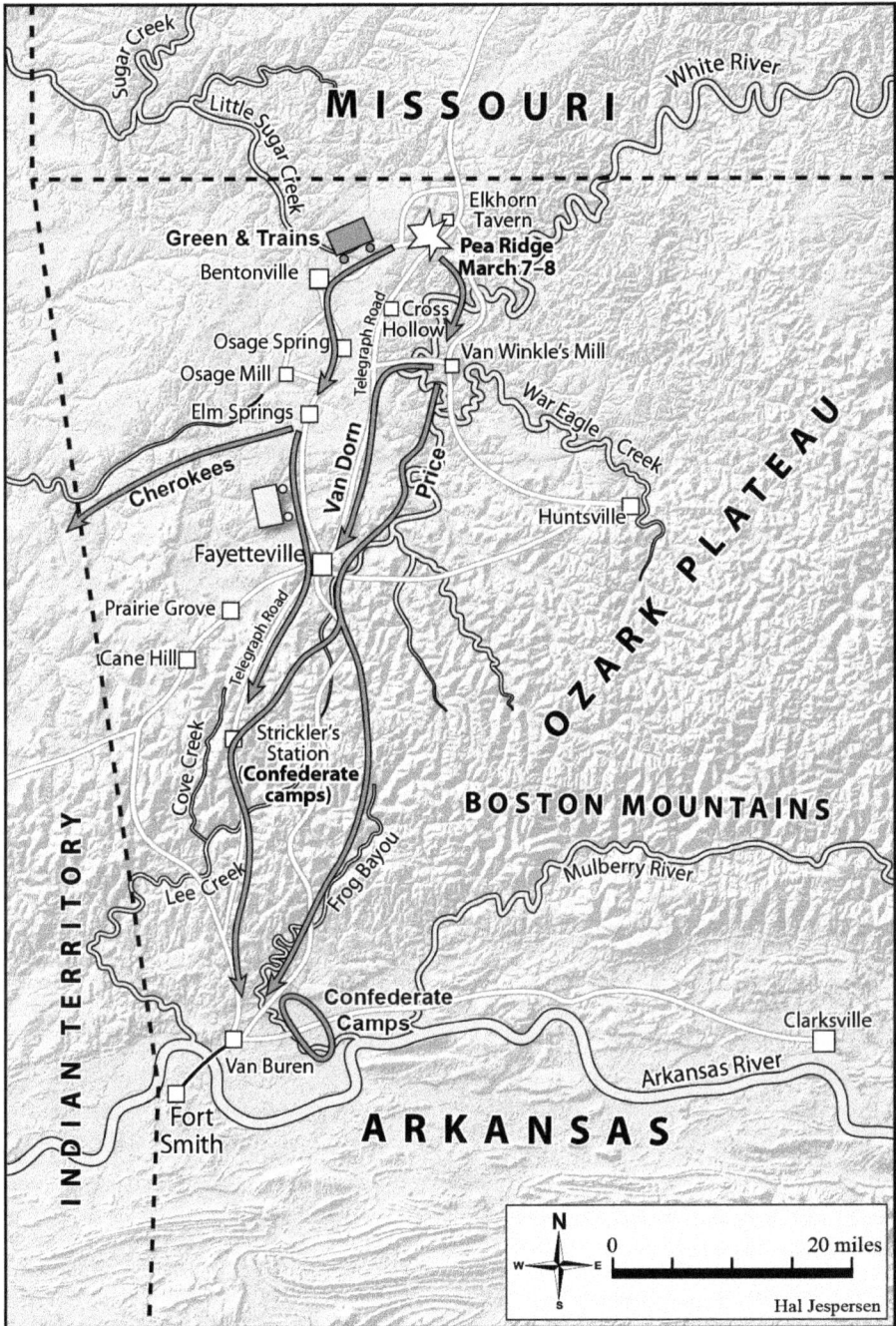

Confederate retreat from Pea Ridge to the Arkansas River Valley on March 8–15. *Courtesy of Hal Jespersen.*

instead of going around to join Van Dorn and Price at Elkhorn Tavern, further adding to Green's forces. Now, as they approached the battlefield, Green commanded at least three thousand men, almost one-fourth of the remaining Confederates on the field.

Sometime after 10:00 a.m., as the train toiled along the Detour, General Green's messenger returned from Van Dorn with news of the retreat, as well as orders to fall back through Bentonville and save the supply train. More confused than ever, Green obediently turned the wagons around and headed west. By that evening, he had managed to get through to Elm Springs. Some Federal cavalry followed as far as Bentonville the next day but were easily turned back by Green's rear guard.[133]

With the troops retreating north up Telegraph Road getting the attention of the Federals around the tavern, Franz Sigel saw his chance to get his troops out of what he still considered a precarious situation. Sigel asked and received permission to pursue the Confederates north with most of his First and Second Divisions. Curtis assumed that he meant to just follow them a few miles and then return, but Sigel would march his men—fully half of Curtis's army—almost to Keetsville, Missouri, and then call for his supply wagons and suggest that the rest of the army join them. Curtis's angry reply was that he had no intention of falling back and ordered Sigel to get his troops back to Pea Ridge immediately.

While all of this was going on, troops from the Fourth Division, on the right of Curtis's line, were finding evidence that the main body of Van Dorn's army had gone east out on Huntsville Road. Elements of the Third Illinois Cavalry and Colonel Dodge's Fourth Iowa followed for a while, finding the road strewn with discarded equipment and the surrounding woods full of stragglers, but the Federals did not pursue very far and were slow to realize that Van Dorn's main body had gone this way.[134]

While Samuel Curtis and about half of his victorious army were settling in around Elkhorn Tavern, collecting the wounded and rounding up prisoners, Earl Van Dorn and Sterling Price were leading what was left of Price's Missouri divisions plus several units of McCulloch's division to the southeast. It was, in fact, several miles before most of the troops realized that the army was retreating instead of just moving to a different position. When this became known, there was a lot of anger, since most of the men didn't feel that they had been beaten. As one Louisiana soldier put it, "[I]t was clear enough that there had been a shameful piece of bungling and mismanagement, and the discontent and clamor became general and everyone was disgusted."[135]

The Civil War Fight for the Ozarks

The sentiment of many of the Missouri soldiers was voiced by Brigadier General James Rains of the State Guard Eighth Division, who, when ask by his soldiers if they had lost the battle, answered, "By God, nobody was whipped at Pea Ridge but Van Dorn!" Unfortunately, Rains was overheard by Van Dorn himself and was put under arrest.[136]

The Confederates camped at Van Winkle's Mill the first night, and since they had no supply wagons of their own—and since this was, for many soldiers, the third day without food—everybody was out foraging. As one soldier put it, "Every living biped and quadruped was immediately killed and eaten." Another said, "[A] pinch of salt would, that night, have been worth a general's ransom."[137]

The part of the Confederate army that retreated with Van Dorn and Price was in a sorry shape. The men were exhausted and hungry, generally destitute of tents, blankets or overcoats to cope with the winter weather and separated from their supply train in a primitive and sparsely settled country. Now they faced a trek back to the Arkansas River Valley over some of the wildest and most rugged terrain between the Alleghenies and Rockies. General Van Dorn left them the next day, taking a small group, striking out southwest through Fayetteville and arriving at Van Buren two days later. This left the wounded General Price to attempt to lead the survivors out of the Boston Mountains.

William Watson was a sergeant in the Third Louisiana and part of a group sent by Van Dorn back to Pea Ridge under a flag of truce to arrange an exchange of prisoners. Another group was sent back to bury the dead. Returning from that mission to what was left of his regiment, Watson summed up the predicament of his Louisiana soldiers, who now had to follow the Missouri troops on the retreat, very well:

The distance to Van Buren in a direct line was about 90 miles. This would have been nothing if there had been anything like a good road and tolerable weather, but to reach it, we might have to traverse twice that distance. The White River and its many tributaries was in the way. There were no roads or bridges; the country was mostly hills covered with scrub oaks, rocks, rivers and creeks…and so poor, as some of the men expressed it, that turkey buzzards would not fly over it…the weather had now set in worse than the dead of winter—cold biting winds, sleet, frost, and snow. Price's army had preceded us…clearing the country of everything that could be eaten by man or beast, even to the last acorn, which seemed to be the only thing the country produced.[138]

Even the Confederates who were fortunate enough to retreat back the way they had come—through Bentonville and Fayetteville—were a sad-looking lot. Reverend William Baxter, who had watched them come through in high spirits on the way to the battle, now watched them stream back past his home in Fayetteville: "[N]ow the army was a confused mob, not a regiment, not a company in rank, save two regiments of cavalry which, as rear guard, passed through near sundown. The rest were a rabble-rout… everyone seemingly animated by the same desire to get away."[139]

For over a week, thousands of men in hundreds of small groups trudged over the crest of the Boston Mountains and down into the Arkansas River Valley. While some found their way to Telegraph Road near Strickler's Station and from there into Van Buren, many more followed Frog Bayou down to the Arkansas River, where the Confederate winter camps were located. Some were fortunate enough to meet supply wagons sent by Van Dorn along Frog Bayou near the site of present-day Mountainburg, while others had to struggle all the way to the Confederate camps. There, finally, they found a good supply of provisions and began to recover from one of the most trying ordeals that any group of Civil War soldiers would face outside of life in a prison camp.

One of the few bright spots for the Confederate army came a week after the battle when Captain John Good of Texas and Captain William Wade of Missouri arrived, having pulled forty pieces of artillery over one hundred miles through the Ozarks. Good wrote to his wife the next day, "Our retreat was to Van Buren in the most miserable weather over the most miserable roads it has ever fallen the lot of poor mortallity [sic] to travel, but we arrived safe…yesterday about 12 noon, men and horses starved nearly to death."[140]

The Pea Ridge Campaign was over. Samuel Curtis kept his army in the Pea Ridge area for ten days after the battle, transporting the wounded, resupplying and satisfying himself that the Confederates were truly gone. They then fell back up Telegraph Road to Keetsville, Missouri, having stripped the country around Pea Ridge of all available forage. Van Dorn's army settled in around Van Buren, Arkansas, and slowly regained something of its strength and organization. Officially, the Federals suffered 1,384 casualties, with Eugene Carr's Fourth Division suffering fully half the losses during its seven-hour stand at Elkhorn Tavern. Confederate casualties during the battle were never officially listed but must have been about 2,000, with hundreds more lost during the approach to Pea Ridge and the retreat back to Van Buren.[141]

Once back at Van Buren, General Van Dorn begin planning another grand offensive, but on March 25, he received orders from General Albert Sidney Johnston to bring his army to Corinth, Mississippi, where Johnston was massing troops to strike a Federal army concentrating across the state line at Pittsburg's Landing. By moving Van Dorn's army east of the Mississippi, the Confederacy essentially abandoned northern Arkansas and southern Missouri to the Yankees for the foreseeable future. Sidney Johnston, however, would not live to see Van Dorn's army. He was killed at Shiloh on April 6, before any of the Arkansas troops could arrive. General Thomas Hindman would raise another army in northwest Arkansas later in 1862, with the intent of threatening Missouri again, but would be defeated at Prairie Grove in December, effectively ending any Confederate threat for the next two years.

Samuel Curtis was nominated for promotion to major general on March 27 and that same day learned that his daughter, Sadie, had died of typhoid in St. Louis. Curtis would move his army east, following Van Dorn's movements at first, and then he would strike south through eastern Arkansas, arriving at Helena on the Mississippi River on July 12. In September, Major General Curtis was given command of the Department of Missouri but was soon reassigned to the Department of Kansas and Indian Territory because his abolitionist remarks had offended Governor William Gamble. It was a purely political move, with President Lincoln quoted as saying, "One of them had to go, and as I could not remove the governor, General Curtis lost his command."[142]

The Pea Ridge Campaign pitted a young, dashing and aggressive cavalryman and Indian fighter against an older engineer and administrator—both of them fighting their first major engagement. The cavalryman and Indian fighter rushed to the battle, pushing his men and trusting more to speed, good fortune and bravado than to organization and planning. In doing so, he exhausted his men, divided his army and lost control of his logistics. His men fought valiantly but could not overcome the odds that haste, mismanagement and bad luck stacked against them.

The old administrator and engineer, on the other hand, kept control of his army, moved aggressively but with solid planning and refused to be intimidated by his opponent's superior numbers. During the battle, he did not panic when faced with the enemy's bold and unexpected moves but rather maneuvered promptly to meet them, turning his entire army completely around in the middle of the fight. Curtis was also blessed with solid subordinates like Eugene Carr, whose Missouri and Iowa men held Curtis's right flank against twice their numbers on March 7, as well as Peter Osterhaus and Jefferson Davis, who defeated Ben McCulloch's division at Leetown.

The Battle of Pea Ridge was fought in an obscure place, across the mighty Mississippi from what were considered the more important theaters of the war, and it was overshadowed by the Federal victories at Fort Henry and Fort Donelson two weeks earlier, and then by Shiloh a month later. Seldom in the war, however, did the control of so much vital territory depend on the outcome of one battle. Though none knew it at the time, Samuel Curtis's victory at Pea Ridge ensured Federal control of Arkansas, north of the river, and the entire state of Missouri for the rest of the war—more than eighty-five thousand square miles.

The cannons are now silent, and the smoke has long drifted away, but the battlefield at Pea Ridge remains much as it was 150 years ago. The Boston Mountains over which so many exhausted men toiled still retain much of their wild character, and the Telegraph Road can still be followed in many places. The men who fought on what was then a remote and little-known field were every bit as committed and as brave as any who fought east of the Mississippi. In fact, many of them would later fight in Mississippi, Tennessee and Georgia but would never forget the time in the heart of the Ozarks, where they suffered and bled and starved and froze and "saw the elephant" for the first time.

The Commanders

THE FEDERALS

SAMUEL RYAN CURTIS

After Pea Ridge and his later campaign into eastern Arkansas, Curtis was given command of the Department of Kansas and Indian Territory. In October 1863, his son, Major H. Zarah Curtis, was killed by Quantrill's Raiders. In October 1864, Curtis defeated Sterling Price a second time at Westport, Missouri. After the war, Curtis helped with treaties with the Plains Indians and with the Union Pacific Railroad. Curtis died the day after Christmas 1866 in Council Bluffs, Iowa.

FRANZ SIGEL

After the battle, Sigel served in the Eastern Theater but would never again equal the success he had on the second day at Pea Ridge. In 1864, he was relieved of his command. After the war, he worked as a newspaper editor and received a number of political appointments over the years. Sigel died in New York City in 1909.

ALEXANDER ASBOTH

After Pea Ridge, Asboth continued to serve for the rest of the war in Mississippi, Kentucky and Florida, where he was wounded again in the Battle of Marianna in September 1864. After the war, he was appointed United States minster to Argentina and Uruguay. Asboth died in Buenos Aires in 1868.

APPENDIX A

Eugene Asa Carr

Carr continued to serve for the rest of the war, ending as a brevet major general. After the war, he remained in the army, serving in the Indian Wars. Carr retired in 1893 after forty-three years in the army. The next year, he received the Medal of Honor for his service at Pea Ridge thirty-four years earlier. Eugene Carr died in 1910 in Washington, D.C.

Jefferson Columbus Davis

After Pea Ridge, Davis commanded a division in Mississippi and then went on sick leave. On September 29, 1862, Davis shot and killed his superior officer, Major General William "Bull" Nelson, following an argument at the Galt House in Louisville, Kentucky, but with the help of Major General Horatio Wright avoided conviction for murder because of the need for experienced commanders in the field. After the war, Davis was the first commander of the Department of Alaska and served in the Modoc War. Davis died in Chicago in 1879.

Peter Joseph Osterhaus

Osterhaus served for the rest of the war, becoming a major general and commanding the XV Corps in Sherman's army during the March to the Sea. After the war, Osterhaus was appointed the United States consul in Lyons, France, but eventually moved back to his native Germany. Peter Osterhaus retired in 1905 and lived to see the beginning of World War I, dying in Duisburg, Germany, in 1917, the oldest pentioner on the U.S. Army list and the last surviving senior commander from Pea Ridge.

The Confederates

Earl Van Dorn

After Pea Ridge, Van Dorn was ordered to bring his army across the Mississippi River but did not arrive in time for the Battle of Shiloh. Later that year, Van Dorn fell into disfavor after his poor performance at Corinth in October, but partially redeemed himself with a very successful cavalry raid behind Grant's lines at Holly Springs, Mississippi, in December. By March 1863, Van Dorn was in Middle Tennessee, commanding the cavalry on General Bragg's left flank. While there, Van Dorn, a well-known ladies' man, made the acquaintance of Jessie McKissack Peters, the young wife of a local doctor, and rumors began to circulate of an affair between the two. On May 7, 1863, Van Dorn was in his office at his headquarters in the home of Martin Cheairs at Spring Hill, Tennessee, when Dr. James Peters, Jessie's husband, entered and shot Van Dorn in the head. A local historian later commented that "Earl Van Dorn just took one too many late night buggy rides." Because his home in Port Gibson, Mississippi, was in Federal hands at the time, Van Dorn was buried on property owned by his wife's family near Mobile, Alabama. In 1899, he was finally moved home to Port Gibson.

STERLING PRICE
After the battle, Price and his Missouri troops went with Van Dorn across the Mississippi. After the Battle of Corinth, Price asked for leave and went to Richmond but failed to impress President Davis, who thought the Missouri general "the vainest man I ever met." In late 1864, Price led a campaign back into Missouri but was defeated once again by Samuel Curtis at Westport—present-day Kansas City. Instead of surrendering at the end of the war, Price led a group into Mexico, but his health failed and he returned to Missouri, where he died on September 29, 1867. His funeral was said to be the largest in the history of St. Louis up to that time.

ALBERT PIKE
After Pea Ridge, Pike stayed in Arkansas and Indian Territory but did not get along with his new commander, Major General Thomas Hindman, and resigned in July 1862. After the war, Pike became known as an authority on Freemasonry, publishing *Morals and Dogma of the Ancient and Accepted Scottish Rite of Freemasonry* in 1871. Pike died in Washington, D.C., in 1891.

LOUIS HEBERT
After being captured at Pea Ridge, Hebert was exchanged and served in Mississippi and North Carolina until the end of the war. After the war, Hebert returned to Louisiana, taught school and published a newspaper in St. Martin's Parish. Louis Hebert died in 1901, his remains now resting in Cecilia, Louisiana.

LEWIS HENRY LITTLE
A regular army officer before the war, Little commanded the First Missouri Brigade at Pea Ridge. It was Little's men who captured Elkhorn Tavern on March 7. After the battle, Little came east with Van Dorn's army and commanded the First Division of Price's army at Iuka, Mississippi.

Late in the afternoon on September 19, 1862, while sitting on his horse next to General Price during the battle, Little was hit in the head and killed instantly.

Lawrence Sullivan Ross

Although only a major at Pea Ridge, "Sul" Ross went on to command his regiment—the Sixth Texas Cavalry—and then a brigade under General Steven D. Lee. Ross then commanded a brigade under Forrest in Hood's Tennessee Campaign. Ross participated in 135 engagements during the war without being seriously injured. Returning to Texas, Ross served as a sheriff, a delegate to the 1875 Constitutional Convention and a state senator. In 1886, Ross became the nineteenth governor of Texas. When Ross, a Democrat, decided to run for a second term in 1888, the Republican Party declined to even field a candidate. Upon leaving the governorship, Ross became the president of the Agricultural and Mechanical College of Texas (which became Texas A&M), a post that he held until his death on January 3, 1898.

Appendix B

Order of Battle

Pea Ridge, Arkansas
March 7–8, 1862

Information courtesy of Pea Ridge National Military Park and excerpted from William L. Shea and Earl J. Hess, Pea Ridge: Civil War Campaign in the West.

Key: (k) killed; (w) wounded; (c) captured; MOH, Medal of Honor.

FEDERAL ARMY OF THE SOUTHWEST
BRIGADIER GENERAL SAMUEL R. CURTIS
First and Second Divisions—Brigadier General Franz Sigel

First Division—Colonel Peter J. Osterhaus
    First Brigade—Colonel Peter J. Osterhaus
        Twenty-fifth Illinois—Colonel William N. Coler
        Forty-fourth Illinois—Colonel Charles Knobelsdorff
        Seventeenth Missouri—Major August H. Poten
    Second Brigade—Colonel Nicholas Greusel
        Thirty-sixth Illinois—Colonel Nicholas Greusel
        Twelfth Missouri—Major Hugo Wangelin
    Artillery
        Fourth Independent Battery, Ohio Light Artillery—Captain Louis Hoffman
        Welfley's Independent Battery, Missouri Light Artillery—Captain Martin Welfley

Second Division—Brigadier General Alexander S. Asboth (w)
    First Brigade—Colonel Fredrick Schaefer
        Second Missouri—Lieutenant Colonel Bernard Laibolt
        Fifteenth Missouri—Colonel Francis J. Joliat
    Artillery
        First Missouri Flying Battery—Captain Gustavus M. Elbert
        Second Independent Battery Ohio Light Artillery— Lieutenant
            William B. Chapman
    Not Brigaded
        Third Missouri—Major Joseph Conrad (Companies B, C and E present)
        Fourth Missouri Cavalry (Fremont Hussars)—Major Emeric Meszaros
        Fifth Missouri Cavalry (Benton Hussars)—Colonel Joseph Nemett

Third Division—Colonel Jefferson C. Davis
    First Brigade—Colonel Thomas Pattison
        Eighth Indiana—Colonel William P. Benton
        Eighteenth Indiana—Lieutenant Colonel Henry D. Washburn
        Twenty-second Indiana—Lieutenant Colonel John A. Hendricks (k)
            Major David W. Daily Jr.
        First Battery Indiana Light Artillery—Captain Martin Klauss
    Second Brigade—Colonel Julius White
        Thirty-seventh Illinois—Lieutenant Colonel Myron S. Barnes
        Fifty-ninth Illinois (formally Ninth Missouri)—Lieutenant Colonel
            Calvin H. Frederick
    Battery A Second Illinois Light Artillery (Peoria Battery)—Captain
        Peter Davidson
    Not Brigaded
        First Missouri Cavalry—Colonel Calvin A. Ellis

Fourth Division—Colonel Eugene A. Carr (w) MOH
    First Brigade—Colonel Grenville M. Dodge (w)
        Fourth Iowa—Lieutenant Colonel John Galligan (w)
        Thirty-fifth Illinois—Colonel Gustavus A. Smith (w)
            Lieutenant Colonel William P. Chandler (c)
        First Independent Battery Iowa Light Artillery—Captain Junius A.
            Jones (w)
            Lieutenant Virgil A. David
        Third Illinois Cavalry—Major John M. McConnell

Appendix B

Second Brigade—Colonel William Vandever
    Ninth Iowa—Lieutenant Colonel Francis J. Heron (w/c) MOH
        Major William H. Coyl (w)
    Twenty-fifth Missouri (Phelps's Independent Missouri Regiment)—
        Colonel John S. Phelps
    Third Independent Battery, Iowa Light Artillery (Dubuque
        Battery)—Captain Mortimer M. Hayden

Headquarters Units
    Twenty-fourth Missouri—Major Eli W. Weston (Provost Marshal)
    Third Iowa Cavalry—Colonel Cyrus Bussey
    Bowen's Missouri Cavalry Battalion—Major William D. Bowen

CONFEDERATE ARMY OF THE WEST
MAJOR GENERAL EARL VAN DORN

McCulloch's Division—Brigadier General Benjamin McCulloch (k)
      Brigadier General James M. McIntosh (k)
      Colonel Elkanah Greer
  Hebert's Infantry Brigade—Colonel Louis Hebert (c)
      Colonel Evander McNair
    Third Louisiana—Major Will F. Tunnard (c)
      Captain W.L. Gunnells
    Fourth Arkansas—Colonel Evander McNair
        Lieutenant Colonel Samuel Ogden
    Fourteenth Arkansas—Colonel William C. Mitchell (c)
    Fifteenth Arkansas—Colonel Dandridge McRae
    Sixteenth Arkansas—Colonel John F. Hill
    Seventeenth Arkansas—Colonel Frank A. Rector
    First Arkansas Mounted Rifles (dismounted)—Colonel
      Thomas J. Churchill
    Second Arkansas Mounted Rifles (dismounted)—Colonel
      Benjamin T. Embry
    Fourth Texas Cavalry Battalion (dismounted)—Major
      John W. Whitfield
  McIntosh's Cavalry Brigade—Brigadier General James M. McIntosh (k)
    Third Texas Cavalry—Colonel Elkanah Greer
      Lieutenant Colonel Walter P. Lane
    Sixth Texas Cavalry—Colonel B. Warren Stone

Ninth Texas Cavalry—Colonel William B. Simms (w)
    Lieutenant Colonel William Quayle
Eleventh Texas Cavalry—Colonel William C. Young
First Arkansas Cavalry Battalion—Major William H. Brooks
First Texas Cavalry Battalion—Major R. Phillip Crump

Artillery
    Hart's Arkansas Battery—Captain William Hart
    Provence's Arkansas Battery—Captain David Provence
    Gaines's Arkansas Battery—Captain James J. Gaines
    Good's Texas Battery—Captain John J. Good
Pike's Indian Brigade—Brigadier General Albert J. Pike
    First Cherokee Mounted Rifles—Colonel John Drew
    Second Cherokee Mounted Rifles—Colonel Stand Watie
    First Choctaw and Chickasaw—Colonel Douglas H. Cooper
    First Creek Mounted Rifles—Colonel Daniel N. McIntosh
    Welch's Texas Cavalry Squadron—Captain Otis G. Welch

Unassigned (remained with the supply train under Brigadier General Martin Green)
    Nineteenth Arkansas—Lieutenant Colonel P. R. Smith
    Twentieth Arkansas—Colonel George W. King

Price's Division—Brigadier General Sterling Price (w)

Confederate Units
First Missouri Brigade—Colonel Henry Little
    Second Missouri—Colonel John Q. Burbridge
    Third Missouri—Colonel Benjamin Revis (k)
        Lieutenant Colonel James A. Pritchard
    Wade's Missouri Battery—Captain William Wade
    Clark's Missouri Battery—Captain S. Churchill Clark (k)
        Lieutenant James L. Farris
    First Missouri Cavalry—Colonel Elijah Gates
Second Missouri Brigade—Colonel William Y. Slack (k)
        Colonel Thomas H. Rosser
    Hughes's Missouri Infantry Battalion—Colonel John T. Hughes
    Bevier's Missouri Infantry Battalion—Major Robert S. Bevier
    Rosser's Missouri Infantry Battalion—Colonel Thomas H. Rosser

Landis's Missouri Battery—Captain John C. Landis
Jackson's Missouri Battery—Captain William Lucas
Riggins's Missouri Cavalry Battalion—Colonel George W. Riggins
Third Missouri Brigade—Colonel Colton Greene
  Partially organized battalions and companies of both infantry and
  cavalry just transferring into Confederate service.

Headquarters Units
  Cearnal's Missouri Cavalry Battalion (Price's Escort)—Lieutenant
    Colonel James T. Cearnal (w)
    Major T. Dodd Samuels

Missouri State Guard Units
  Second Division—Brigadier General Martin E. Green
    Various unidentified infantry and cavalry units
    Kneisley's Battery—Captain James W. Kneisley
  Third Division—Colonel John B. Clark Jr.
    First Infantry—Major John F. Rucker
    Second Infantry—Colonel Congreve Jackson
    Third Infantry—Major Robert R. Hutchinson
    Fourth and Fifth Infantry—Colonel J.A. Poindexter
    Sixth Infantry—Lieutenant Colonel Quinton Peacher
    Tull's Battery—Captain Francis M. Tull
  Fifth Division—Colonel James P. Saunders
    Various unidentified infantry and cavalry units
    Kelly's Battery—Captain Joseph Kelly
  Sixth Division—Major D. Herndon Lindsay
    Various unidentified infantry and cavalry units
    Gorham's Battery—Captain James C. Gorham
  Seventh and Ninth Divisions—Brigadier General Daniel M. Frost
    Various unidentified infantry and cavalry units from Frost's
    and Brigadier General James H. McBride's divisions
    Guibor's Battery—Captain Henry Guibor
    MacDonald's St. Louis Battery—Captain Emmett MacDonald
  Eighth Division—Brigadier General James S. Rains
    First Infantry—Colonel William H. Erwin
    Second Infantry—Lieutenant Colonel John P. Bowman
    Third Infantry—Lieutenant Colonel A.J. Pearcy
    Fourth Infantry—Lieutenant Colonel John M. Stemmons
    Shelby's Cavalry Company—Captain Joseph O. Shelby
    Bledsoe's Battery—Lieutenant Charles W. Higgins

Notes

Prologue

1. Earl Van Dorn to his wife, January 18, 1862, Arthur B. Carter, *The Tarnished Cavalier* (Knoxville: University of Tennessee Press, 1999), 42.
2. The details of Earl Van Dorn's early life and military career leading up to his appointment as the commander of the Trans-Mississippi Department come from Carter's *Tarnished Cavalier*, with additional information from William L. Shea and Earl J. Hess, *Pea Ridge: Civil War Campaign in the West* (Chapel Hill: University of North Carolina Press, 1992), 20–22.
3. Shelby Foote, *The Civil War: A Narrative*, vol. 1 (New York: First Vintage Books Edition, 1986), 277–81; Shea and Hess, *Pea Ridge*, 5–7.

Chapter 1

4. William L. Shea, "Semi Savage State," from *Civil War in Arkansas: Beyond Battles and Leaders*, ed. Anne J. Bailey and Daniel E. Sutherland (Fayetteville: University of Arkansas Press, 2000), 86.
5. Ibid., 87–88.
6. Ibid., 89.
7. Arkansas Civil War, http://arkansascivilwar.com/about/chapter1.aspx.
8. Michael B. Dougan, *Confederate Arkansas* (Tuscaloosa: University of Alabama Press, 1976), 63.
9. The information on McCulloch's background before the war is from Thomas W. Cutrer, *Ben McCulloch and the Frontier Military Tradition* (Chapel Hill: University of North Carolina Press, 1993), 200.
10. Ibid., 198.

11. William H. Tunnard, *A Southern Record: The History of the Third Regiment, Louisiana Infantry* (Baton Rouge, LA: self-published, 1866), 28. Author's collection.
12. Cutrer, *Ben McCulloch and the Frontier Military Tradition*, 208–9.

Chapter 2

13. Louisiana had been admitted eight years earlier but was not entirely a part of the Louisiana Purchase—only the part west of the river plus the city of New Orleans.
14. Phil Gottschalk, *In Deadly Earnest* (Columbia: Missouri River Press, 1991), 9.
15. Details on the Missouri Compromise and the Kansas/Nebraska Act may be found at these websites: http://en.wikipedia.org/wiki/Missouri_Compromise and http://en.wikipedia.org/wiki/Kansas%E2%80%93Nebraska_Act. Information on Missouri leading up to the firing on Fort Sumter and the events that finally brought it into the war come primarily from Gottschalk, *In Deadly Earnest*, chapter 1, and Albert Castel, *General Sterling Price* (Baton Rouge: Louisiana State University Press, 1968), chapter 1.

Chapter 3

16. *The War of the Rebellion: A Compilation of the Official Records of the Union and Confederate Armies*, 128 vols. (Washington, D.C.: Government Printing Office, 1880–1901), series 1, vol. 3, 611. (Hereafter referred to as *OR*. All references are from series 1.)
17. *OR*, vol. 3, 622–23.
18. Cutrer, *Ben McCulloch and the Frontier Military Tradition*, 223.
19. For Price's version, given by one of his supporters, see Castel, *General Sterling Price*, 37. For General N.B. Pearce's version, see Cutrer, *Ben McCulloch and the Frontier Military Tradition*, 221. For McCulloch's version, see *OR*, vol. 3, 745.
20. Gottschalk, *In Deadly Earnest*, 28.
21. For those interested in more details about the Battle of Wilson Creek, thirty-nine after-actions reports are contained in the *OR*, vol. 3, beginning at page 53. Although it is doubtful that the Southern forces in front of General Lyon's position ever numbered much more than ten thousand, Major Sturgis stated in his report that he believed he was opposed by at least twenty thousand (Report of Sturgis, *OR*, vol. 3, 67). Throughout the war, both sides consistently overestimated their opponent's strength.

Chapter 4

22. *OR*, vol. 3, 672–73.
23. Cutrer, *Ben McCulloch and the Frontier Military Tradition*, 255.
24. By the time McCulloch reached Richmond, Price had written to Jefferson Davis that "the obstacles in the way of the successful prosecution of the war in this state" were due "mainly, if not altogether to the conduct of General McCulloch," Cutrer, *Ben McCulloch and the Frontier Military Tradition*, 268. Little wonder that McCulloch felt it necessary to defend himself in person.

25. *OR*, vol. 3, 743. For those wishing to read McCulloch's much more detailed report of his actions before and after Wilson Creek and his reasons for them, see his report, immediately following the one cited here, written after his arrival in Richmond and dated December 22, 1861, in *OR*, vol. 3, 743ff.

26. Cutrer, *Ben McCulloch and the Frontier Military Tradition*, 270.

CHAPTER 5

27. *OR*, vol. 8, 462.

28. Ibid., 471–72. Both Sigel's and Curtis's brigadier general commissions dated from May 17, 1861. In fact, there were thirty-four brigadier generals in the Federal army whose date of rank was May 17. If two officers had the same date of rank, as was the case with Sigel and Curtis, seniority was determined by the order in which they were listed in the official Army Register. In the listing of the thirty-four brigadier generals promoted on May 17, Samuel Curtis was number nineteen, while Franz Sigel was number twenty-five. Curtis was, in fact, senior to Sigel, if only by a small technicality.

29. Steven D. Engle, *Yankee Dutchman* (Baton Rouge: Louisiana State University Press, 1993), 1–47.

30. For more detail on Sigel and Halleck's conflict and the political fallout, see Engle, *Yankee Dutchman*, 90–98.

31. Gottschalk, *In Deadly Earnest*, 36, 42.

32. Shea and Hess, *Pea Ridge*, 10–13.

33. See the Order of Battle in Appendix B.

34. *OR*, vol. 8, 478–79.

35. Henry Halleck to Samuel Curtis, *OR*, vol. 8, 506.

CHAPTER 6

36. Shea and Hess, *Pea Ridge*, 29.

37. Halleck to Curtis, February 15, 1862, *OR*, vol. 8, 556.

38. Report of Major William D. Bowen, *OR*, vol. 8, 269.

39. Shea and Hess, *Pea Ridge*, 33.

40. Ibid., 34.

41. Curtis to Halleck, February 16, 1862, *OR*, vol. 8, 558.

42. Tunnard, *Southern Record*, 123.

43. Three weeks later, many of them would fight—and some would die—around that tavern.

44. Dr. Washington Lafayette Grammage, *The Camp, the Bivouac, and the Battlefield* (Little Rock: Arkansas Southern Press, 1958), 22–23; Tunnard, *Southern Record*, 119; Gottschalk, *In Deadly Earnest*, 52; Shea and Hess, *Pea Ridge*, 37–38.

45. Tunnard, *Southern Record*, 123–24.

Chapter 7

46. Curtis's army numbered a little more than twelve thousand when he began his pursuit of Price from Lebanon Missouri, but after having to drop off troops to run and guard his supply line, by the time he reached Little Sugar Creek, he had just over ten thousand men, Shea and Hess, *Pea Ridge*, 52.
47. *OR*, vol. 8, 63.
48. Grammage, *The Camp, the Bivouac*, 23.
49. William Baxter, *Pea Ridge and Prairie Grove* (Fayetteville: University of Arkansas Press, 2000), 20.
50. Tunnard, *Southern Record*, 124–25. Major Tunnard here is mistaken in saying that the retreat began on Tuesday morning. It began on the morning of the nineteenth, which was a Wednesday.

51. Grammage, *The Camp, the Bivouac*, 23; Tunnard, *Southern Record*, 125; Baxter, *Pea Ridge and Prairie Grove*, 24–25.
52. Baxter, *Pea Ridge and Prairie Grove*, 26.
53. Ibid., 27–28; *OR*, vol. 8, 69–70.
54. Michael A. Hughes, "Wartime Gristmill Destruction in Northwest Arkansas and Military Farm Colonies," from *Civil War in Arkansas: Beyond Battles and Leaders*, 34; Shea and Hess, *Pea Ridge*, 53.

Chapter 8

55. Carter, *Tarnished Cavalier*, 47.
56. Colonel Dabney H. Maury, Van Dorn's chief of staff, stated that Van Dorn's group made the entire trip to the Confederate camps on horseback, but Shea and Hess state that the group found an ambulance on the way to Van Buren and that Van Dorn rode in it for most of the rest of the campaign, Dabney H. Maury, *Recollections of the Pea Ridge Campaign*, vol. 2 (Richmond, VA: Southern Historical Society Papers, July–December 1876), 183; Shea and Hess, *Pea Ridge*, 56.
57. Maury, *Recollections of the Pea Ridge Campaign*, 185.
58. Gottschalk, *In Deadly Earnest*, 54.
59. Shea and Hess, *Pea Ridge*, 54–55. Major "Sul" Ross would go on to become a brigadier general and finish the war serving under Nathan Bedford Forrest at Franklin and Nashville. After the war, he went home to Texas and, some years later, served two terms as governor.
60. Shea and Hess, *Pea Ridge*, 58–59.
61. Colonel Dabney H. Maury to General Albert Pike, *OR*, vol. 8, 764.
62. William Watson, *Life in the Confederate Army* (Baton Rouge: Louisiana State University Press, 1995), 283.
63. Curtis to Sigel, March 3, 1862, *OR*, vol. 8, 583.
64. Tunnard, *Southern Record*, 130.
65. Shea and Hess, *Pea Ridge*, 60.

Chapter 9

66. Grammage, *The Camp, the Bivouac*, 23.
67. For more details of the Confederate march and the incident at Osage Springs, see Shea and Hess, *Pea Ridge*, 60–64.
68. Ibid., *Pea Ridge*, 69–76; Report of Sigel, *OR*, vol. 8, 208–211.
69. Shea and Hess, *Pea Ridge*, 67; Report of William Vandever, *OR*, vol. 8, 266.

Chapter 10

70. Report of Van Dorn, *OR*, vol. 8, 283.
71. Shea and Hess, *Pea Ridge*, 82; Ross to D.R. Tinsley, March 13, 1862. Copy from Pea Ridge National Military Park, abbreviated as NMP.
72. Report of Colonel Eugene Carr, *OR*, vol. 8, 262.
73. This was Private Welch, Company M, Third Illinois Cavalry, Report of Major Eli Weston, *OR*, vol. 8, 271.
74. Reports of Major General Earl Van Dorn, *OR*, vol. 8, 281ff.
75. Report of Captain Robert W. Fyan, *OR*, vol. 8, 274; Report of Major D. Todd Samuels, *OR*, vol. 8, 329.
76. Reports of Major Eli W. Weston, *OR*, vol. 8, 270ff; Shea and Hess, *Pea Ridge*, 88–89.
77. Report of Brigadier General Samuel Curtis, *OR*, vol. 8, 199; Shea and Hess, *Pea Ridge*, 90.
78. Shea and Hess, *Pea Ridge*, 159.

Chapter 11

79. Shea and Hess, *Pea Ridge*, 93; Report of Weston, *OR*, vol. 8, 271.
80. Shea and Hess, *Pea Ridge*, 151.
81. Report of Colonel Eugene Carr, *OR*, vol. 8, 259.
82. William Y. Slack is often listed as a brigadier general at Pea Ridge, but he was, in fact, still a colonel when he was mortally wounded on March 7. His formal commission as a brigadier general in the Confederate army was awarded posthumously dating from April 12, 1862.

Chapter 12

83. Report of Osterhaus, *OR*, vol. 8, 217.
84. Shea and Hess, *Pea Ridge*, 96.
85. Watson, *Life in the Confederate Army*, 293.
86. Letter from John J. Good to his wife, March 11, 1862, copy from Pea Ridge NMP Archives.
87. Diary of Henry Dysart, Third Iowa Cavalry, copy from Pea Ridge NMP Archives.
88. Shea and Hess, *Pea Ridge*, 99–101.

89. Report of Colonel Cyrus Bussey, Third Iowa Cavalry, *OR*, vol. 8, 235.
90. Shea and Hess, *Pea Ridge*, 102.

CHAPTER 13

91. Information on the placement of units comes from Shea and Hess, *Pea Ridge*, map on page 108.
92. Mary Bobbitt Townsend, *Yankee Warhorse: A Biography of Maj. Gen. Peter Osterhaus* (Columbia: University of Missouri Press, 2010), 58.
93. Report of Colonel Nicholas Greusel, *OR*, vol. 8, 227.
94. Cutrer, *Ben McCulloch and the Frontier Military Tradition*, 302–4; Shea and Hess, *Pea Ridge*, 110–11.
95. Cutrer, *Ben McCulloch and the Frontier Military Tradition*, 303–4; Shea and Hess, *Pea Ridge*, 110–11. Most accounts say that McCulloch was carrying a Maynard rifle, but Cutrer maintained that it was a new and somewhat experimental Morse rifle that used metallic cartridges. Before the war, McCulloch had an interest in the company.
96. Shea and Hess, *Pea Ridge*, 114.

CHAPTER 14

97. Shea and Hess, *Pea Ridge*, 119–20.
98. The Twenty-second Indiana had been temporarily attached to Colonel Osterhaus and had come on the field with Colonel Greusel's brigade but was originally part of Davis's division. The Twenty-second Indiana now reverted to Davis's command and, along with the Eighteenth Indiana, was sent to the east to attack the Confederates' left flank in Morgan's Woods.
99. Watson, *Life in the Confederate Army*, 294.
100. Ibid., 294–95.
101. Shea and Hess, *Pea Ridge*, 136.
102. Report of Greer, *OR*, vol. 8, 293ff; my brief version of the action around Oberson's Field is loosely taken from Shea and Hess, *Pea Ridge*, 94–146, and Townsend, *Yankee Warhorse*, 56–60, as well as passages from Tunnard, Watson and the *OR*, cited in the text.

CHAPTER 15

103. *OR*, vol. 8, 261; Shea and Hess, *Pea Ridge*, 172–73.
104. Report of Rosser, *OR*, vol. 8, 312. Colonel Slack would die from his wound two weeks later, not knowing that his promotion to brigadier general had been approved by Richmond to date from April 12.
105. Report of William Vandever, *OR*, vol. 8, 267; Shea and Hess, *Pea Ridge*, 175–76.
106. Report of Colonel Eugene Carr, *OR*, vol. 8, 260.

CHAPTER 16

107. Shea and Hess, *Pea Ridge*, 168.
108. Report of Captain Albert Jenks, Company A (Cavalry), Thirty-sixth Illinois, *OR*, vol. 8, 230.

CHAPTER 17

109. Ross to D.R. Tinsley, March 13, 1862, copy from Pea Ridge NMP Archives.
110. Shea and Hess, *Pea Ridge*, 183.

CHAPTER 18

111. Shea and Hess, *Pea Ridge*, 186.
112. Jacob Platt, as quoted in Shea and Hess, *Pea Ridge*, 186.
113. Report of Colonel Grenville Dodge, *OR*, vol. 8, 263–64.
114. Ibid., 264.
115. Report of Eugene A. Carr, *OR*, vol. 8, 261. For his actions that day, Herron would receive the Medal of Honor.
116. My brief version of the last stages of the fight around Elkhorn Tavern comes from Shea and Hess, *Pea Ridge*, 185–205, and the Reports of Colonel Eugene Carr, Colonel William Vandever, Colonel Grenville Dodge, General Sterling Price, Colonel Henry Little and Colonel Thomas Rosser, contained in *OR*, vol. 8.

CHAPTER 19

117. Shea and Hess, *Pea Ridge*, 207–8.
118. Grammage, *The Camp, the Bivouac*, 27.
119. Memoirs of A.M. Payne, copy from the Pea Ridge NMPArchives.
120. Report of General Martin Green, *OR*, vol. 8, 317; Report of Colonel Cyrus Bussey, *OR*, vol. 8, 232.

CHAPTER 20

121. Shea and Hess, *Pea Ridge*, 216–20; Report of General Samuel Curtis, *OR*, vol. 8, 201–2.
122. Shea and Hess, *Pea Ridge*, 225–28; Report of Colonel Henry Little, *OR*, vol. 8, 309–10. Colonel Little witnessed the artillery exchange from his position in the Confederate line.
123. John J. Good to his wife, March 11, 1862, copy from Pea Ridge NMPArchives.
124. Report of General Franz Sigel, *OR*, vol. 8, 214.
125. Report of Colonel Thomas Rosser, *OR*, vol. 8, 313.
126. Reports of Colonel W.N. Coler, Twenty-fifth Illinois, and Colonel Charles Knobelsdorff, Forty-fourth Illinois, *OR*, vol. 8, 221ff.
127. Report of Colonel Henry Little, *OR*, vol. 8, 310.

128. Engle, *Yankee Dutchman*, 115.
129. Report of Colonel Henry Little, *OR*, vol. 8, 310. Captain Samuel Churchill Clark was the grandson of explorer William Clark.
130. Shea and Hess, *Pea Ridge*, 251–52.
131. Ibid., 252–53.

CHAPTER 21

132. These were the Nineteenth and Twentieth Arkansas Regiments.
133. Report of General Martin Green, Second Division, Missouri State Guard, *OR*, vol. 8, 317.
134. Shea and Hess, *Pea Ridge*, 257.
135. Watson, *Life in the Confederate Army*, 311.
136. Shea and Hess, *Pea Ridge*, 260.
137. Tunnard, *Southern Record*, 145; Watson, *Life in the Confederate Army*, 314.
138. Watson, *Life in the Confederate Army*, 319–20.
139. Baxter, *Pea Ridge and Prairie Grove*, 46–47.
140. Captain John J. Good to his wife, March 16, 1862, copy from Pea Ridge NMPArchives.
141. Shea and Hess, *Pea Ridge*, 270–71.
142. Geoffrey Perret, *Lincoln's War: The Untold Story of America's Greatest President as Commander in Chief* (New York: Random House, 2004), 266.

Index

INDEX

About the Author

James R. Knight is a graduate of Harding University, class of 1967. He spent five years as a pilot in the United States Air Force flying the C-130E and thirty-one years as a pilot for Federal Express, the last twenty years as a McDonnell Douglass DC-10 captain.

In the early '90s, he began researching a historical incident in his hometown and published his first work, an article in the *Arkansas Historical Quarterly*. In 2003, Eakin Press published his biography of Bonnie and Clyde titled *Bonnie and Clyde: A Twenty-first-Century Update*. In 2007, he published the story and correspondence of a Confederate cavalryman titled *Letters to Anna*. This is his third work in the Civil War Sesquicentennial Series, having written *The Battle of Franklin* in 2009 and *The Battle of Fort Donelson* in 2011.

James R. Knight retired from Federal Express in 2004 and lives in Franklin, Tennessee, where he works part time as a historical interpreter for the Battle of Franklin Trust. When not encouraging visitors at the Carter House to relive some moments of the Battle of Franklin, he collects historical documents and artifacts and occasionally drives his restored 1934 Ford V-8. He and his wife, Judy, have three children and six grandchildren.

www.ingramcontent.com/pod-product-compliance
Lightning Source LLC
Chambersburg PA
CBHW060804100426
42813CB00004B/944